TAKING THE FEAR OUT OF FLYING

Maurice Yaffé

David & Charles

For Francesca – and for all those who had
a fear of flying and the courage to
overcome it

British Library Cataloguing in Publication Data

Yaffé, Maurice
    Taking the fear our of flying –
    1. Fear of flying   2. Self-care, Health
    I. Title   II. Series
    616.85'225   RC1090

    ISBN 0-7153-9030-9
    ISBN 0-7153-9047-3   Pbk

First published in hardback
by David & Charles, June 1987
Published in paperback, March 1988

Reprinted August 1988, 1992

Printed in Great Britain
by Billings Ltd, Worcester
for David & Charles
Brunel House Newton Abbot Devon

Distributed in the United States by
Sterling Publishing Co, Inc,
387 Park Avenue South, New York, NY10016 – 8810

Contents

Introduction

Reliable estimates suggest that apprehension or feelings of fear about flying – worry about what might happen to you and/or the plane – is widespread. Perhaps as many as one in two of the adult population are affected, depending upon how rigidly this anxiety is defined. Statistics indicate that about ten per cent of people *avoid* flying for this reason alone. Considering about one billion people around the world fly annually this represents substantial distress, suffering and inconvenience to the individuals concerned, their families, friends and colleagues, and it can have major consequences for both personal relationships and career prospects. On the very rare occurrences when there is an accident, the media let us all know, and the same applies to disasters which occur involving sea crossings, ski lifts and trains. We never hear about the *good* news. Over the past ten years I have developed effective, practical individual and group courses for dealing with air travel anxiety; this book was written so that relevant information, techniques and exercises can reach a wider audience.

After a general overview of the subject in Chapter 1, normal and abnormal reactions during flight are described in Chapter 2. This is followed in Chapter 3 by a self-assessment of symptoms and a guide to the techniques that are appropriate for overcoming your specific concerns. Next, in Chapter 4, the theory and principles of flight are explained, since many people do not understand how large objects like aircraft manage to leave the ground and stay in the air.

Turbulence – in particular – is covered thoroughly, since this seems to upset many anxious passengers. The five main procedures for bodily relaxation are detailed in Chapter 5, and these are complemented in Chapter 6 by an explanation of how to defuse the worry and negative thoughts associated with flying.

Chapter 7 offers advice on how to create an environment on the ground to simulate relevant flying experiences so that you can practise your coping strategies, and my cabin simulator is described along with those on which pilots train. Chapter 8 explains how to overcome pitfalls and difficulties that may have developed in practising the routines, and the essence of the two-day intensive seminar I run in London for this problem is presented. Chapter 9 gives practical advice about what to do, what to listen to and look out for on your next flight, with explanations of the sequence of plane noises and movements.

I strongly recommend that you read the chapters in sequence first and then go into more detail regarding the exercises and routines relevant to you. Set yourself specific goals and targets based on your assessment profile and practise these every day – taking a flight is the final practice session. If possible, go through the exercises with a friend or partner who can help you to monitor your progress, and discuss with them ways of dealing with practical difficulties.

I am indebted to British Airways for their encouragement and co-operation over the past ten years, without which neither the Seminar nor book are likely to have developed. The collaboration has been a happy one, and I would particularly like to thank Dr Frank Preston, pilots Captain Hugh Dibley and Jock Lowe, and members of Air Traffic Control at London Heathrow airport (Gordon Morehouse and Geoff Bullock). Emily Jacob has been my co-therapist on the Seminar from the beginning and her support and insights have been invaluable. I am grateful to Graham Tarrant for his continued encouragement and enthusiasm in the preparation of this book, especially at times when I seemed to have lost my passion for it in the face of more immediate demands. However, my IBM-AT computer and WordPerfect software made the task of editing the manuscript a pleasure.

Perhaps in the next century someone will need to write a sequel on the fear of inter-stellar flight or orbital trips. By digesting this volume, it might not be necessary.

Maurice Yaffé
York Clinic,
Guy's Hospital, London

1
Fear of Flying

. . . my fingers (and toes) turn to ice, my stomach leaps upward into my rib cage . . . for one screaming minute my heart and the engines correspond as we attempt to prove again that the laws of aerodynamics are not the flimsy superstitions which, in my heart of hearts, I know they are.
I happen to be convinced that only my own concentration (and that of my mother – who always seems to expect her children to die in a plane crash) . . . keeps this bird aloft. I congratulate myself on every successful takeoff, but not too enthusiastically because it's also part of my personal religion that the minute you grow overconfident and really relax about the flight, the plane crashes instantly. Constant vigilance, that's my motto . . . OK, I tell myself, we seem to be off the ground and into the clouds but the danger isn't past . . . This may well be where we go screaming down in thousands of flaming pieces. So I keep concentrating very hard, helping the pilot . . . fly.

Erica Jong, FEAR OF FLYING

This early utterance by Isadora, the central character in Erica Jong's best-seller *Fear of Flying*, crystallises the concern many people have about flying: the unpleasant feeling of rising panic and overwhelming anxiety and a desperate attempt to control it. Her prevailing mood of 'cautious pessimism' revolves around trying to keep the aircraft in the sky by sheer concentration and undiluted attention, and she sees it as *her* responsibility – and not that of the flight crew – to take-off successfully, for which she takes the credit. Were she to take a passive role, the plane would inevitably fall like a stone to the ground. For Isadora, the loss of control, relaxing, and letting the pilot get on with his job of flying the plane is equivalent to inviting death to enter by the front door.

Comments by several well-known but apprehensive fliers provide further insights into understanding the nature of this twentieth-century problem. In spite of hundreds of presidential campaign flights, Ronald Reagan was convinced that he 'held the plane up in the air by sheer willpower'; Muhammad Ali, when asked on television what he was most frightened of, replied: 'Flying. That's the only thing that terrifies me. I'm flying all the time and I feel it's time for one to crash. I don't control the plane. Some pilot does. Say we're between America and England. And the engines stop. Now even if it gets down there without the engines, how am I gonna find my life-raft? And even if I do, how are they gonna see me in the dark? And what happens if a shark comes along and rubs against it . . .?' Furthermore, in 1979 John Heilpern reported in *The Observer* that 'when the Pope arrived at Mexico City Airport and, upon emerging from his plane, kissed the tarmac, people were rightly moved. They know the feeling,' he said, because 'the Pope couldn't believe he'd made it.' And the main reason Claus von Bulow, the Danish-born son of a Nazi playwright, travelled the world acting as the late J. Paul Getty's agent is that his boss was terrified of flying; after having flown through several tornadoes in 1942 Getty never took another flight. This even prevented him from attending his son George's funeral in Malibu, California, thirty-one years later. Another multi-millionaire financier, Huntingdon Hartford, the developer of Paradise Island in the Bahamas, also refuses to fly for similar reasons.

Stuntman Evel Knievel, who in his dramatic career made over five hundred motorcycle jumps over rows of cars and other objects (including live animals!), sustaining injuries that led to him having a substantial number of his bones pinned together, always used to *drive* across the United States. He claimed that he did not want to give anyone an opportunity to kill him before he killed himself; for the same reason he disliked driving fast. Geoff Capes, an ex-Olympic British shot putter, also avoided flying for what he describes as safety

12

reasons and in 1976 went to the Montreal Olympics by land and sea rather than going by air with the rest of the team; just like the international golfer Neil Coles who always travelled to tournaments the same way.

Comedian Bob Newhart, who several years ago made a satirical recording about air travel anxiety, entitled 'The Grace L. Ferguson Airline', describes himself as the 'King of the white knuckles brigade,' who, like many others, has 'a couple of drinks before, a couple during the flight – and then I sit there and suffer.' He even failed to attend a White House function because it would have meant him having to fly there. Actress Glenda Jackson detests flying and claims that her reaction to it is probably the only thing about which she is irrational. For years, Tony Curtis had it expressly written into his contracts that flying was one activity which he would not do. Years previously, apparently, he had been on a flight which almost crash-landed, and he took the view from that time on that flying was particularly dangerous.

Nate Cott and Stewart Kampel, co-authors of *Fly Without Fear**, provide a formidable list of well-known people who admit to a fear of flying, and who articulate their concern graphically. They include William F. Buckley, Jnr, who is reminded every time he flies that 'We are committing an egregious affrontery upon the laws of nature', and Mike Royko, a Pulitzer Prize-winning writer, who

> wouldn't walk into an airplane if it was riveted to the earth. For five thousand years people never flew. Some very civilised men never got more than a foot or two off the ground. Beethoven, Buddha, Plato, Shakespeare, Don Juan, King Tut, and Lenny da Vinci all did their things without once having a stewardess plump their pillows. They got where they were going. But today, if you say you don't fly, you are considered strange.

*H. Regnery & Co, Chicago, 1973

13

Cott and Kampel report that the closest Royko gets to aircraft is when they fly so low over his home that the stewardess could hand him a drink – if his fists weren't clenched. Royko gives some insight into how his apprehension developed:

A long time ago, I rode in airplanes. But that was before I figured out what was really happening. It occurred to me that I was in a metal container that was five miles above the earth, moving at 600mph, ten miles/minute, a mile every six seconds. I closed my eyes and pictured myself in a thin suit of armour, running 600mph smack into a brick wall. The thought upset me. Then I thought of myself in an aluminium box, being dropped off a cliff five miles above a sidewalk. That sickened me. When I staggered off that plane, I vowed I'd never again go 600mph in a metal container. And I haven't.

Even Isaac Asimov, the doyen of science fiction writers, dislikes air travel. He was questioned at a literary dinner as to whether he envied Neil Armstrong for having been the first man to set foot upon the moon. 'Absolutely not,' he retorted, 'I never fly, from sheer cowardice.' Fellow writer of fiction, Irving Wallace, refuses to fly because of his terror of falling, and the late Glenn Gould would not travel by jet plane because he was unable to tell by looking out of the window whether the engines were working. Another famous concert pianist, the Russian Emil Gilels, becomes apprehensive in flight if there is any movement or noise he cannot explain; and André Previn keeps his anxiety about air travel going by avoiding lifts and planes whenever possible, situations that make him feel panicky. He is reported to have told a stewardess during a particularly turbulent part of the flight, while muzak was being played over the sound system: 'Look, I don't care if there's only one chance in a million that we go down. I don't want to die to Lawrence Welk.'

On the other hand, there are some people who are happiest

while travelling by air. To quote Samaritans' founder, Chad Varah: 'The minute I get into a plane I'm home. When you stay one, two or three days in each place and then move on to another country, another set of duties and people, you can become disoriented unless you touch base after each one. The minute I get on board an aeroplane and sit in my favourite place – window seat, second row, left-hand side if I can get it – I relax, I say "Oh, it's nice to be home".' The interesting relationship between fear and courage will be discussed in the next chapter.

Anxiety about air travel is a very common problem, although most people do not feel as uncomfortable as some of those mentioned above. It is estimated that over thirty million people in Britain and the USA want or need to fly but remain either earthbound or terrified in the air. The Association of European Airlines (AEA) conducted a survey in 1974 designed to investigate passengers' requirements and experiences of scheduled intra-European services, and found that 32 per cent answered affirmatively to the statement: The thought of flying scares me a little. This is despite the fact that, over the past few years, flying has become one of the most convenient, comfortable and safe ways to travel, even with the continuing problem of terrorism; moreover, the introduction of lower air fares, especially across the Atlantic, has made it both accessible and attractive to a considerable number of people. In fact, in 1981 alone, 743 million individuals worldwide took scheduled flights – the equivalent of the combined populations of the USA, USSR *and* virtually the whole of Western Europe – and millions more took non-scheduled ones. The comparable figure for the UK is 21.4 million or 39 per cent of the population of the British Isles, which rises to 63 per cent if one includes non-scheduled flights too. The busiest airport in the world in 1985 was Chicago's O'Hare, which dealt with nearly 50 million passengers; London's Heathrow came fourth in the table with over 31 million.

Clearly many people fly, but that comes as no consolation to the apprehensive flyer, who often protests that it is a risky

15

and dangerous business. However, international air safety statistics in relation to this considerable traffic inform us that the chances of being involved in an accident (not necessarily a fatal one) on a large public transport aircraft is one in a million (this is an average figure – the American accident rate is 0.5 per million flights and the rest of the world 1.5 per million flights) – the equivalent of flying every day for ninety-five years! In fact, as Cliff Parker points out in his book *How to avoid flying**, 'More people in the world are kicked to death by donkeys than die in flying accidents'. But that never occurs to anyone. In other words, flying, relative to other forms of transport, is very safe; yet air travel anxiety is very widespread. So extensive that in the USA alone it costs the domestic air travel industry over twenty-one million one-way trips each year – an overall nine per cent reduction in air travel – which in 1978, according to research conducted by the Boeing Company, represented $1.6 billion lost revenue.

The purpose of this book is to help you understand and pinpoint the source of your anxiety about flying, and to learn appropriate techniques for coping with this stress. But first of all it is helpful to put the anxiety that people experience in relation to air travel in perspective with respect to other commonly expressed fears. According to the London *Sunday Times* (7 October 1973), a market research organisation in the United States asked a cross-sectional, representative sample of three thousand inhabitants: 'What are you most afraid of?' Respondents were allowed to name more than one fear if they wished to do so. Eighteen per cent answered that flying was something about which they were most afraid, which came eighth in the overall list. The seven more prevalent fears were: speaking before a group (41 per cent); heights (32 per cent); insects and bugs, financial problems, and deep water (all 22 per cent); sickness and death (both 19 per cent). Further down the list came darkness and lifts (8 per cent) and escalators (5 per cent). Significantly more women than men

*New English Library, 1982

expressed fears, apart from the item about financial problems. Although flying *per se* was stated as *most* fear-provoking by 18 per cent, it is likely that a good number of people who are anxious about air travel may simply have responded affirmatively to the height and lift items, as these are common fear-inducing situations in many who actively dislike flying.

In one of the few studies on how fears and phobias are distributed in the community, Stewart Agras, an American psychiatrist, and his colleagues† at the University of Vermont, in 1969 (still the most comprehensive study of its kind) reported on the basis of interviews with 325 randomly selected persons that flying is, along with going to the dentist, the fourth most widespread common fear and affects 198 out of 1000 in the population – following snakes (390), heights (307), and storms (211). For comparison, common fears with a lower prevalence include fear of injury (182), illness (165), death (161), enclosures (122), journeys alone (74), and being alone (44). In those where the *intensity* of fear of flying is greater 109/1000 are affected, and only snakes (253) and heights (120) affect people more in this way. The frequency of mild phobia in this sample was 77/1000 and of severe phobia 2.2/1000, none of which was related to flying. Moreover, none of their comparison clinical phobic series of fifty cases expressed a concern about flying; their patients' concerns comprised agoraphobia (50 per cent), injury and illness (34 per cent), death and crowds (8 per cent), animals (4 per cent), heights and darkness (both 2 per cent). Results confirm the view that the frequency of phobias, as in other conditions in psychiatric practice, does not correspond closely to how common they are in the general population.

Another study, reported in the American magazine *Psychology Today*, involved data collected in New Orleans from 214 persons in restaurants and shopping centres, and found a fear of flying rate of 21 per cent. The survey was

†Agras S., Sylvester D. and Oliveau D., *Comprehensive Psychiatry*, Vol 10, 1969

extended to include air travellers at New Orleans International Airport and an overall fear of flying figure of 13 per cent was obtained. In both this and the Vermont study air travel anxiety was shown to be twice as prevalent among women compared to men (11 per cent v 27 per cent in Vermont; 14 per cent v 28 per cent in New Orleans [city sample] and 7 per cent of the men and 20 per cent of the women [airport sample]). In general, anxiety and phobias are more common in women than in men. Why should this be so?

Three explanations have been put forward by Professor Isaac Marks of the London Institute of Psychiatry. He contends that: 'Three mechanisms may act together to produce the lower incidence of fears in normal men. First is the biological tendency for men to be stronger, more aggressive, and less fearful, which is partly due to androgens. Next, from early childhood onwards, environmental pressure is stronger on boys than on girls to act fearlessly, which may eventually lead them to be more fearless. Finally men may be less willing to admit to fear than women.' Apart from men's biological propensity to be assertive and aggressive, one might predict that the frequency of anxiety and phobias between the sexes may become more equal if the masculist movement catches on.

Although specific therapy programmes for air travel anxiety have only been available for the past ten years, concern about this issue was expressed by the President of American Airlines as far back as 1937, when an advertising campaign with the headline 'Why Dodge This Question: Afraid To Fly?' was launched in the national magazines of the time. The text read as follows:

We know that fear keeps many people from enjoying the advantage of air transportation. So why should we be silent on this subject? American Airlines, Inc. has carried more than a million passengers. These people travel by air for the same reason they use the telephone, send telegrams, and ride in elevators. It is a quicker, more modern, more efficient way to accomplish what they want to do.

Are airlines safer than railroads? You can find intelligent people to take both sides of the argument. Whether you fly or not does not alter the fact that no form of transportation – on the ground, on the water, or in the air – can guarantee its passengers absolute immunity from danger.

This whole subject of fear about flying can be summed up as follows: PEOPLE ARE AFRAID OF THE THINGS THEY DO NOT KNOW ABOUT. You would be equally afraid of trains if you had never ridden on one. As soon as you become acquainted with air transportation, your fear will be replaced by your enjoyment of the many advantages of air travel.

That's all very well, but as we shall see in the next chapter, this message is unlikely to comfort the fearful flier, for information about emotive issues is rarely processed impartially. Those who hold strong negative views about, and unfavourable reactions towards, air travel will probably accept at face value any negative statements about it – this would fit into their preconceived ideas, in contrast to the non-anxious flier who is likely to put any new knowledge about it into some kind of positive perspective. This is one of the principal reasons why flying is such a problem today for so many people: air travel is construed as a threat to the individual's status quo over which they believe they have either little or no control. In other words, flying is a negative stress.

Stress, defined as any change to which one must adjust, is unavoidable in today's world. Although flying, to the fearful flier, and illness or injury, are occurrences we label as negative and unwanted, stressful events can be positive, such as winning an athletic competition, falling in love or being promoted at work. But research by Dr Hans Selye, a Canadian physician, and others, has shown that the pleasantness or otherwise of the occasion, called the 'stressor', is not important; what matters is the intensity of demand it makes upon you to adapt. Selye has demonstrated that the body responds in three stages to a stressor; in the first, known as the Alarm Stage, the body acknowledges the source(s) of stress and hormones are released from the endocrine glands which produce raised heart beat, increase in respiration rate and pupil size, the release of sugar into the blood and a slowing down of digestive processes. These changes enable the brain to obtain more oxygen, which facilitates thinking ability; the eyes can see better, hearing becomes more acute, and muscles tense to meet the challenge. All of these lead to confrontation of the stressor (fight) or escape (flight), depending upon which reaction seems most appropriate.

In the second (Resistance) stage the body deals with the consequences of the stressor, but physical preparedness will be maintained should its presence continue. If the body is unable to obtain a respite from the biochemical changes that occur during the initial stage, the regulatory centres of the brain are likely to overact. The third (Exhaustion) stage follows if the stressor is applied for long enough; chronic stress wears people down and eventually out, and along the way stress disorders may develop, including peptic ulcers, circulatory problems, asthma, and cardiac irregularities. Eventually the body runs out of available energy supplies. Transient elevated blood pressure can under these circumstances develop into chronic hypertension, a condition shared by over twenty-five million Americans, half of whom are unaware that they have it.

As we cannot live a life without stress, we have to learn how to handle it. It is possible by reading this book to change negative stress to 'neutral' stress, and to counteract your air travel anxiety by learning how to relax: the brain centres which control the biochemical and physiological changes when you contemplate and experience a flight can be trained to slow down. But we need to focus initially on the differences between normal and abnormal responses to air travel.

2
Normal and Abnormal Reactions to Air Travel

Nothing in life is to be feared, it is only to be understood.
MADAME CURIE

Imagine being on a scheduled flight at night in Africa and expecting to land in a few minutes, when the captain announces that the runway lights have been switched off. What do you feel?

You are cruising at 41,000ft, suddenly one of your engines loses full power and the other three begin to operate with reduced thrust. The aircraft starts to plummet at 15,000ft per minute; the landing gear comes down and the doors are ripped off in the process. At 11,000ft the pilot begins to regain control, and by 9,000ft he pulls out of the dive. What are your reactions?

You have just boarded a flight in the Middle East and you find yourself sitting next to an Arabic looking young man carrying a case close to his chest, who looks very agitated? What do you conclude?

You take a high speed lift to the thirtieth floor of a tower block on your first visit there and the doors do not open right away? What thoughts go through your head?

There are no absolute standards regarding normal and abnormal reactions to air travel for the airline passenger.

These are determined by the subtle interplay between physical and psychological factors, past experiences and present expectations. Basically, if flying is perceived as a threat and you are unable to exert desirable control over it, then anxiety is likely to result. In the examples presented above, only the second story, which involved a China Airlines Jumbo jet from Taipei to Los Angeles in April 1985, represented a realistic danger to both passengers and crew. This Boeing 747SP dropped six miles in two minutes and in the process practically turned upside down as it rolled to the right, for which there was no good explanation at the time. An hour later the 747 made an emergency landing at San Francisco International airport; a number of passengers and cabin crew were found to have sustained minor injuries during the dive, but there were no fatalities.

On the other hand, the African incident, which occurred on 2 September 1984, when the runway lights at Lusaka International airport were turned off on the instruction of a frustrated (and obviously disturbed) senior government official – happened simply because he could not find a seat on a flight to London! As a result, a Zambia Airways Hawker Siddeley on a scheduled flight from Ndola, carrying a number of people who had seats booked on the London flight, was unable to land and was forced to return to the Copperbelt from where it came. This was, of course, an uncomplicated manoeuvre for the crew without endangering passengers or aircraft, though many of them understandably were extremely annoyed by the inconvenience.

The story from the Middle East was told to me by an anxious woman client afraid of flying, who informed the cabin crew of her concern. It was explained in due course that the man in question was 'simply fearful of flying since he disliked the sensation of being off the ground.' The lift vignette occurred to a claustrophobic patient of mine who was worried that the doors would *never* open, and as in the previous account the situation was construed as threatening. The lift, by the way, is the safest form of transportation today – one of the largest elevator companies, Otis, moves the equivalent of the world's population every *nine* days!

Before we can fully understand the different reactions to air travel, it is necessary to define some of the terms and concepts related to it and to classify the various types and symptoms of anxiety, adaptive and otherwise.

Definitions

The terms *fear*, *anxiety* and *phobia* are often used imprecisely and interchangeably, in spite of the desirability of keeping them separate, and this also applies to related concepts, including *panic* and *superstition*.

The word *fear* derives from the Old English *faer*, meaning 'sudden calamity' or 'danger'. In modern usage it generally connotes the likely occurrence of an unwanted event perceived as having negative consequences, about which a person has anticipatory concerns; ie the emphasis is on *cognitive appraisal* rather than an *emotional reaction*. Fear is normal in situations where there is a real or specific danger, like being a passenger in a taxi where the driver is determined to get you to the airport on time regardless of heavy traffic and treacherous weather, and has obvious survival value in leading you either to avoid such situations or to handle them more adaptively, as in the previously mentioned China Airlines incident. Fear can even be an enjoyable experience for the sensation seeker (eg free-fall parachutist or microlight enthusiast) and also useful – up to a point – in providing necessary arousal levels for learning, say, how to fly a light aircraft.

In contrast, *anxiety*, which comes from the Latin *anxius*, 'a condition of agitation and distress', and *angere*, which means 'to choke or strangle'; a similar Greek word refers to 'press tight or strangle'. Anxiety is an unpleasant emotional reaction, usually accompanied by a variety of physical symptoms including palpitations, perspiration, tension, shakiness, and increased pulse rate.

In other words, fear involves the *evaluation* of an event as

23

threatening, whereas anxiety refers to the emotional *reaction* given that appraisal. When someone says that they are afraid of flying they are usually referring to something which might occur in the future – when the fear may be described as latent – but it is activated if they decide to take a flight or even think of doing so; that is, exposure to the feared event can be actual or imaginary, physical or psychological.

Phobia is a term that originates from the Greek word *phobos*, meaning 'flight', and was taken from one of their gods, Phobos, who apparently evoked considerable fear (and panic) in his enemies. It is an extreme kind of fear, out of proportion to what is required in the situation, that can neither be explained nor reasoned away; it is largely beyond voluntary control and leads to avoidance of confrontation. In phobic anxiety of air travel, the anxiety reaction occurs only in contact with flying, but the person may also be phobic about other related or even unrelated situations – eg lifts, underground trains and high buildings, or spiders and snakes. The phobic individual generally acknowledges that his or her reaction is inappropriate and unnecessary, and recognises that others are unlikely to react the same way about air travel or whatever it is he or she is phobic about.

The principal distinction between an everyday fear and a phobia is the extent to which it interferes with your life. If you have no intention or need of travelling by air, a fear of being off the ground is unlikely to disrupt your daily routine. However, if you dislike the height aspect of flying you probably would not travel to the top of high buildings for work or leisure purposes, which could well interfere with your life. In this case, the fear is more properly described as a phobia.

The word *panic* also has a Greek etymology and was similarly adopted from a deity, this time called Panikos, who it was claimed created a feeling of terror among his adversaries. The term in contemporary usage refers to attacks which are characteristic of *panic disorder* (see Chapter 3); these attacks are characteristically sudden and unexpected, coupled with intense apprehension, fearfulness or sense of terror, and are often associated with feelings of impending doom. Physical changes accompany these features and include hyperventilation (or over-breathing), palpitations, chest pain or discomfort, choking or smothering sensations, and fear of losing control or going crazy.

Superstitions are collective beliefs about luck (both good and bad) that are shared by a cultural group and for which there is no objective evidence in support. For example, in Nepal, the world's only Hindu kingdom, there is an ancient belief that spilled blood can be a blessing and for the past twenty-seven years, since its formation, Royal Nepal Airlines has consecrated each of its aircraft by sacrificing a goat to Durga, the Hindu goddess of destruction. A representative of the airline was reported in the *Guardian* in November 1986 as saying that they sprinkled fresh goat's blood on the wheels of the aircraft 'to make sure that it has its share of blood, and will not have any accident and seek human blood.'

Other common superstitious beliefs among fearful flyers are that it is dangerous to travel on the thirteenth day of any month, or sit in Row 13 of an aircraft, and that so long as you grip the arm rests of your seat throughout the flight and do not go to sleep, the plane will not 'fall out of the sky'. Or that if you were to stand up and walk down the aisle, the aircraft would instantly tip over onto its side and plummet to the ground.

This is a rich area where cognitive therapy – detailed in Chapter 6 – can have considerable impact by teaching you how to modify your irrational ideas.

Obsessions are recurrent, persistent ideas, thoughts, images or impulses, that are unwanted and resisted.

Compulsions are repetitive and deliberate acts that are performed according to certain rules or in a stereotyped manner. They are specifically intended to produce or present some future state of affairs, such as ensuring flight safety or preventing travel accidents, and are either inappropriate or excessive but may afford some temporary relief of tension.

Preoccupations are repeated thoughts or images without the presence of resistance; for example, that you are going to have problems on your next flight.

A typical obsessive rumination about flying that therapists often encounter is where a client feels that a particular flight, say one that a friend or relative is taking, will crash; the compulsive behaviour often linked with this thought is to contact the airline until you know that the plane has definitely reached its destination, to check its progress, to listen to the media news in case there are reports of an accident.

Various expressions have been used to convey 'phobic anxiety about flying' including *aerophobia* or *pterophobia* (from the Greek word for wing) but, as you can see, the problem is a heterogeneous one so no single term can encompass the different varieties.

Fear, courage and fearlessness

The person who is willing to fly although frightened, who experiences a high degree of subjective fear and even some unpleasant bodily reactions, is *courageous* – ie their overt behaviour (travelling by aeroplane) overrides their subjective discomfort. In contrast, people who are prepared to approach an objectively fearful situation (like parachuting) without experiencing subjective fear or unpleasant bodily reactions are best described as being *fearless* rather than courageous. What makes one person courageous and another fearful depends largely upon cognitive factors discussed later in the chapter.

Labelling fear and anxiety

It is possible to label a fear as 'realistic' or otherwise depending on whether it is based on sensible or fallacious assumptions, logical or faulty reasoning, objective or distorted observations. Whereas anxiety, since it refers to an affective response and not to an evaluative process, cannot be deemed to be 'rational' or 'irrational'. Anxiety can be considered a *normal* reaction if it is generated by a realistic threat, so long as it subsides when the danger has passed. It is abnormal if the level of reaction is vastly unequal to both the potential risk and the severity of the considered danger, and if it remains in spite of the absence of actual danger. There is no definitive criterion between normal and unhealthy anxiety, but one might obtain a clue by looking at how common the reaction is amongst others in the individual's cultural or social group. For instance, a traditional Nepalese, knowing that blood had never been sprayed on the wheels of his aircraft, may feel uncomfortable because of shared cultural myths concerning the protection and safety which that act confers. His anxiety would be considered normal, in the same way that one would expect a hot air balloonist to be anxious prior to his first flight.

Let us now see how these mental reactions relate to some of the physical changes that take place in a typical flight situation.

Bodily changes and problems of altitude

Bodily discomfort produced by flying can also be mistaken for anxiety, due to subtle variations in the cabin environment which involve both pressure and oxygen changes. Physically healthy individuals are at no disadvantage, but infirm, debilitated or older passengers may be at risk as a result of the physiological stresses involved. The modern passenger jet operates mainly at cruising altitudes of between 14,000 and 40,000 feet (Concorde up to 60,000ft), depending on distance and routeing and for reasons of efficiency: less fuel is used at higher altitudes due to lower wind resistance, and weather conditions are generally more favourable, affording greater passenger comfort.

Aircraft maintain a comfortable cabin pressure when flying at altitude by drawing in external air, which is then compressed and distributed throughout the cabin. Cabin air, therefore, is not a 'finite quantity contained in cylinders that can run out', as one patient thought. It is completely changed in the cabin every three minutes or so, and thus is always fresh and in unlimited supply.

27

Pressure changes

As a rule, commercial airline cabins are pressurised somewhere between 5,000 and 7,000 feet, for two reasons: as a physiological safety margin for passengers, and because aircrew performance deteriorates at unpressurised altitudes of 8,000ft or more. Pressurisation to sea level is preferable but a much heavier aircraft would be required, and therefore this would not be cost effective. Air at 6,000ft above ground level will, if free to do so, increase in volume by almost one-third because of reduced atmospheric pressure. This also applies to air contained within the body and is responsible for the need to clear your ears during ascent and descent. Not knowing about these changes or what to do about them can be very anxiety-provoking. (The best way of relieving the problem is known as the *Valsalva manoeuvre*: close off the air supply to your nose with one hand and blow strongly against the pressure until you feel air passing through your Eustachian tubes – the pathway that connects ears and throat.)

During ascent expanding gas located in the middle-ear cavity is able to escape via the Eustachian tubes, which produces the familiar 'popping' sensation. Problems can arise on the descent since the air is unable to flow back through this pathway and pressure is directed onto the tympanic membrane, which can be extremely painful. In order to deal with this and equalise the pressure between the middle ear and the atmosphere, simply swallow, yawn, move your lower jaw from side to side, or suck a sweet. Otherwise, try the Valsalva manoeuvre.

You may also notice a slight swelling of your abdomen due to gas expansion, and in your small intestine this is made worse by food and drink (avoid beans, curries, cabbage, carbonated drinks and alcohol – the worst offenders). The problem is compounded because the gas cannot readily escape, compared to that in the stomach or large intestine where flatulence is a prominent symptom.

Oxygen changes

The other important physiological effect of reduced cabin pressure at altitude is a lowering of available oxygen in the atmosphere. A cabin pressurised to 6,000ft will produce a reduction of oxygen in the blood of about three per cent – negligible to a healthy, non-smoking person at rest and relaxed; but for some passengers exposure to such conditions may produce mild hypoxic symptoms – subtle personality changes, lack of judgement, mental confusion (features similar to alcoholic intoxication) – and can lead to the stimulation of cardio-vascular and respiratory compensatory mechanisms, the most common being increased respiration and hyperventilation. Smokers are at a disadvantage because carbon monoxide preferentially displaces oxygen from the haemoglobin molecule in the blood, thereby reducing the amount of oxygen available for release into the tissues. A heavy smoker may already be at an equivalent altitude of several thousand feet while still on the ground at sea level!

The main features of hyperventilation include light-headedness, tingling sensations in hands and feet (paraesthesia), dizziness, palpitations, feelings of unreality and anxiety. For the anxious flyer this can compound a pre-existing disposition, but diaphragmatic breathing exercises are effective in dealing with such symptoms (see Chapter 5). In contrast, the problems of hypoxia can be overcome by the use in flight of supplementary oxygen which is always carried.

A variety of medical conditions require special precautions or planning for air travel and others are contra-indicated (see Appendix I for list and recommendations).

Acceleration changes

Acceleration is the rate of increase of velocity with time, and occurs when the speed or direction of motion of the aircraft changes. This can produce physiological effects which are determined by the magnitude, duration and direction of the acceleration. For the airline passenger these effects are not nearly as extreme as for the military pilot, but they are greater than you are likely to experience from other forms of transport and can be anxiety-provoking if you do not know what to expect. The first sensation of this kind, when the aircraft accelerates down the runway prior to take-off, is being pushed back in your seat – in accordance with Newton's third law of motion (see Chapter 4 for explanation).

During the initial phase of the climb and shortly after the seat-belt sign has been turned off, you might find it difficult to walk along the aisle due to the extra force of gravity being exerted and the angle of the cabin, especially if banking is taking place.

Spacial orientation and disorientation

On the ground, our sense of orientation in space (ie position, attitude and movement) is determined by gravity and the horizon. Information is gleaned from eyes, ears and proprioceptors – receptors or sense organs situated within tissues of the body; but during flight, feedback supplied by these sensory modalities, especially from the inner ear and proprioceptors, may be interpreted incorrectly and evoke anxiety. This occurs often when apprehensive flyers avoid looking out of the window or close their eyes as a way of cutting down flying related cues, and also by resisting banking when the aircraft is turning. Since over eighty per cent of our input is provided from visual sources, it is not surprising that feelings of disorientation can result from misinterpretation of these ambiguous, and sometimes unfamiliar, cues.

Motion sickness

This is a normal reaction of sensory function in response to real or apparent, unknown or unusual, motion stimuli. The prevalence in passengers is very low (much less than one per cent) and does not increase greatly even in severe turbulence (eight per cent). Such extreme conditions are very rare, and would in all probability be avoidable due to radar and meteorological aids. The main features are stomach discomfort, feelings of nausea, sweating and a pale complexion. The con-

30

dition can progress and leads to increased salivation and vomiting (for which a paper bag is provided in the adjacent seat pocket); associated symptoms can include drowsiness, hyperventilation and flatulence.

Stress and anxiety prior to and during a flight can increase the likelihood of its occurrence, but it can be reduced by keeping your head still, closing your eyes, and inclining your seat back as far as it will go.

Noise
Noise – that is, any unwanted sound – is the accompaniment of any flight and can produce stress by increasing bodily arousal, irritability and tiredness, and by making it necessary to concentrate more because of the unwanted interference. Noise while flying is basically due to jet outflow – the inter-action between the aircraft and the air through which it is moving (known as *boundary layer* noise) – aircraft pressurisa-tion, air conditioning and hydraulic systems, and sometimes other passengers (especially returning sports teams and young children who demand attention). Noise varies accord-ing to the type of aircraft, phase of flight and where you are sitting. Subsonic jets are quieter than Concorde (especially the rear cabin), newer planes are quieter than older ones, take-off and landing are noisier than the cruise phase, and the further back in the cabin you travel the noisier it will become. This is one of the reasons why first class is always at the front of an aircraft; the other is the fact that there is less relative movement, due to the yawing effect.

General stresses and strains of flying
Airline advertisements communicate to the public a rather restricted view of what it is actually like to fly. Many discom-forts and inconveniences that occur on every flight are seemingly discounted. The images conveyed are always taken during smooth level flight, usually when delicious looking food is being served, without the aisle blocked by a trolley. No mention is made of the toilets which are invariably engaged

when you want to use them; the changes in angle that the cabin goes through; turbulence; or the level of noise.

These omissions are significant, for a substantial number of passengers find these changes uncomfortable and often feel that their flight experience is extreme, when it is very typical. According to a report in the *Wall Street Journal* in June 1984, it is surprising that

> the indignities of flying don't come up much in conversations with non-fliers, or even with people who say that they used to fly but don't anymore. One hears little or nothing about slow ticket lines, confusing fares, down computers, security checks, five-abreast seating, squalling children, second-rate movies, crummy earphones, blocked aisles, airline food, and the mingled aromas of cigarette smoke and cheap cologne. One hears about terror.

Other impositions include often having to walk long distances in terminal buildings to get to departure gates and fitting comfortably into a restricted seating area if you are tall or overweight.

Fatigue, dehydration and *boredom* can also produce problems in relation to air travel. How often in life do we have to sit in one place for three, four, six or even ten hours plus? Probably nowhere else outside of air journeys. Long journeys are tiring, mainly due to the disruption of biological (circadian) rhythms that affect sleep and digestive processes. These are more marked during night flights and east-west journeys, where a number of time zones are crossed quickly. (For those travelling to Britain, eastbound transatlantic trips are worst, along with westbound flights from the Indian sub-continent.)

Dehydration is a consequence of the cabin pressurisation and reduced oxygen availability at altitude, and is affected adversely by ingestion of alcohol. Congeners – additives to alcohol that make it more stable and also contribute to hangovers – may also make 'jet-lag' worse (ie poorer adaptation to the environment at your destination). So it is recommended that non-alcoholic liquids are consumed intermittently on a long journey to compensate for the loss of water in the body due to atmospheric changes. Boredom is the resultant of continual low stimulation on a long flight and can be anxiety provoking (see Appendix II for one suggestion of how to prevent this happening to you).

It is therefore necessary to redress the balance about the realities of flying so that people can learn what really happens, rather than expect the false image presented in the media.

Reactions to flying when viewed as a threat

When a person perceives flying as dangerous or as a threat, he constantly scans the environment (eg weather conditions) for signs of impending disaster or personal harm. This limits the opportunity for detached, rational and analytical thinking, but automatic protection reactions generally take over. These include specific somatic (bodily) reflexes that produce 'freezing' or seat-gripping behaviour, autonomic changes like diarrhoea and nausea, or panic attacks – that both signal alarm to others that you are distressed or act as a stimulus for you to escape from the situation at the first opportunity. In other words, we make an initial appraisal of the situation and coping possibilities, decide whether there is a definite danger and respond accordingly – ie stay and confront, escape, incubate or 'freeze' or faint. When this occurs the arousal persists for long after your initial concern was stimulated, in addition to the over-reaction in the first place.

Abnormal anxiety reactions, then, comprise an automatic set of bodily responses resulting from the perceived danger of taking a flight, combined with an underestimation of your ability to deal with it effectively.

Symptoms
These can be separated into thoughts (the worry factor), feelings (or mood), behaviour (or action), and physiological (or bodily reactions), which try to cope with the threat.

33

Anxiety problems in relation to air travel, and other situations for that matter, represent a defect in the process for starting and stopping an adaptive response to threat. Perceived inability to cope effectively makes the threat more pronounced, and the symptoms you have indicate what action needs to be taken (see Chapter 3). Many *cognitive symptoms* about air travel are *exaggerated* versions of normal reactions (eg extreme wariness or self-consciousness); other symptoms represent a *suppression* of normal functions (eg confusion, distractability or poor concentration); yet others indicate a *lessening of control* with respect to processes ordinarily controllable, such as loss of objectivity. An example illustrating these features is one client with a history of depression, who expressed feelings of unreality on an aircraft where she disliked 'the sheer space beneath'. For her this was 'a kind of experience of death', and in keeping with these comments her pulse rate was exceptionally low and her extremities were cold. She did not understand the theory of flight, and felt out of control of the situation. These sensory-perceptual disturbances can be explained in terms of an attempt to avoid physiologically what is perceived as life-threatening cognitively. In other words, she threw in the towel.

Thinking difficulties can produce 'tunnel vision' and preoccupation with the threat component of flying, and *emotional reasoning* (see Chapter 3) serves to reinforce the anxious flyer's preconceived ideas about the dangers (internal or external) of air travel, along with associated fears about not being able to cope, losing control, precipitating a mental disorder or heart attack.

Mood changes depend upon the situation but range from edginess to a feeling of extreme terror – eg general uneasiness on booking your ticket which builds up as the flight approaches to a distressing, and perhaps incapacitating level on the day of the journey.

Bodily symptoms depend on the action plan you have worked out: escape or confrontation. This will determine whether an active coping strategy is triggered – ie increased heart rate

34

and blood pressure – or a passive strategy (eg collapse or faint) where breathing is attenuated and other physiological channels of response are slowed down.

Behavioural symptoms vary from total inhibition through restlessness to hyperactivity – perhaps avoidance of a flight or even escape after boarding.

The main concern about air travel can centre around fears of becoming physically unwell (eg triggering a heart attack), mentally unbalanced (eg going mad) or of being an embarrassment to others (eg screaming the aircraft down). Often individuals have not crystallised the catastrophe they feel will occur to them, but the conviction that it will occur is usually strongly held. Each person has a characteristic way of responding to these fears depending upon their mode of response: activation, inhibition or withdrawal.

In *activation*, the person is extremely vigilant for cues relevant to danger, like looking for loose rivets on the wing or checking for fire emanating from the engine, and talks in terms of imminent disaster. The threshold for detection is very low – a frown on the stewardess's face means she knows there is trouble with the aircraft but is not letting on. The emotional status of such a person is variable, heart rate is raised along with blood pressure and sweating and there is an increase in muscular activity, including grimacing, shakiness and often chain-smoking. If there were more room on the aircraft, pacing up and down the aisles could be added to the list.

With *inhibition*, on the other hand, normal thinking and behaviour is disrupted on a flight. Poor recall of important information like the whereabouts of a passport or other travel documents is typical, along with faulty reasoning, limited concentration and general mental inefficiency. In terms of behaviour, there is lack of facial expression and some jerkiness and variability in movements. The *withdrawal* mode of response, which most often occurs in relation to injections and the sight of blood or injury, produces symptoms of weakness and fainting.

Several types of distorted thinking accompany these different modes of expression, including: *catastrophising* – assuming the worst situation will happen given any possibility for an undesirable outcome (eg one change in engine tone or hint of turbulence means your number is up); *selective abstraction* – that is, selecting information that fits in with your preconceived ideas (for instance, picking out reports of aircraft accidents from the newspaper and dismissing the hundreds of successful take-offs and landings that happen every day) to prove the point that flying is dangerous; and *polarised thinking* – interpreting events in dichotomous terms (eg unless a flight can be absolutely guaranteed safe, it must be dangerous). These and other instances of distorted thinking are covered fully in Chapter 3.

In summary, the evaluation of mental and physical reactions to air travel is determined according to whether or not flying is perceived as either threatening or dangerous, and if so, you feel you have the ability to cope with the situation. In such cases, symptoms usually cluster and may be classified into various types; these are discussed in the next chapter along with an indication of how common they are, a description of how to analyse your symptoms, and details of therapeutic alternatives.

3

The Reduction of Fear

To the man who is afraid, everything rustles.
SOPHOCLES

From the previous chapter it can be seen that flying can be both physiologically and psychologically stressful. In contrast to bodily stress, the psychological stress of flying relates to much more than what is happening right now; it can refer either to a distressing flight in the past or to an anticipated one in the future. The perception of threat determines your ability to adapt and cope with the trauma of a previous flight or to prepare effectively for the next one. The present chapter provides practical instructions on how to establish your personal flight stress profile, which will indicate precisely the appropriate combination of information and exercises likely to resolve your difficulties; and so long as this homework is carried out systematically and regularly, future flying need not be a problem.

However, there are many who feel they need to do something about their air travel anxiety, but deny that it is a problem. It only becomes a problem, of course, if it interferes with your life to the extent that the consequences of having it are worse than if you didn't; and only you can decide that. Denial of flying as a threat can prevent you from seeing any positive aspects of it, especially if this is coupled with no hope of feeling differently about it. Thus, it is important to complete the following questionnaires, as they really apply to you at present. Do not expect to feel differently about flying until

37

you have practised the routines recommended for you, *and* taken a flight as the final step in the therapeutic programme.

Pinpointing the specifics of your concerns about flying – which can vary considerably from one person to another – is an important initial phase in coming to terms with the problem. An assessment of your pattern of reactions – thinking, bodily and behaviour changes related to different aspects of air travel (your personal *flight stress profile*) – can be used as an index of your present level of functioning and for comparison purposes after you have put into practice the recommendations that follow. In some cases symptoms cluster into *syndromes*, the most common of which are *panic disorder* and *simple phobia*, and these are discussed subsequently along with how common they are and likely causal influences.

ASSESSMENT

The following questionnaires help you to find out how *you* respond to different aspects of flying and related situations.

1. Anxiety intensity rating

This simple scale allows a useful and rapid measure of subjective discomfort, anxiety or tension, in relation to flying or any other situation. Zero rating implies total relaxation and subjective feeling of comfort, whereas ten – the opposite extreme – indicates the worst panic or sense of terror that you have ever suffered or can conceive of experiencing. Other ratings signify various intermediate levels of discomfort. It can be used at the beginning of an exercise session and again at the end as a measure of discomfort and change over time, and in due course during different phases of a flight.

0	1	2	3	4	5	6	7	8	9	10

Calm,   Moderate   Extreme
relaxed   anxiety   panic, terror

On a day to day basis, it is helpful to make a mental note of your rating, at different times of the day, particularly when you feel any tension, pressure, stress or anxiety.

2. Anxiety in situations related to flying

The questionnaire overleaf includes situations and experiences about which some anxious flyers also feel uncomfortable, and is adapted from the *Fear Survey Schedule* developed in 1973 by Joseph Wolpe, an American psychiatrist.

Indicate for each item the extent of the discomfort you feel by using the scale shown. Do not ignore items which you have not encountered; it is your *feeling* about them that matters. Place a letter 'A' over the rating if you *avoid* that situation.

If you answered any item with a rating of 3 or 4 *and* avoid that situation or experience, then this requires dealing with, for all of these have a potential for disrupting your life outside of flying as well as during air travel. The following breakdown will determine which category of anxiety disorder applies to you, so that you can refer to the appropriate section later in this chapter.

Question No	Category of Disorder
1	Generalised anxiety disorder
2–5	Panic disorder and agoraphobia
6–18	Specific phobias
19–21	Social phobia

If you avoid any of the situations – a formula for keeping problems alive – you will need to confront these in a graded way, least to most anxiety provoking, before you feel better about them. The REDUCTION section later in this chapter will explain how to proceed.

3. Anxiety and stages of air travel

The second questionnaire (page 42) is designed to ascertain how anxious you become in each of the many situations involved in taking a flight. Several brief descriptions of such

	Anxiety Rating				
	Panic, terror	Very anxious	Moderately anxious	Slightly anxious	Calm, relaxed
	4	3	2	1	0

1. General inability to relax.
2. Being alone.
3. Being in a strange place.
4. Large open spaces.
5. Crowds.
6. Looking down from high buildings.
7. Looking down from high ground.
8. Travel by bus.
9. Travel by train.
10. Travel by car.
11. Travel by lift.
12. Travel by cable car.
13. Being strapped in.
14. Confined spaces.
15. Sight of deep water.
16. Fire.
17. Darkness.
18. Falling.
19. Entering room of strangers.
20. Being told what to do.
21. Being judged by others.

TABLE: Anxiety in Flying Related Situations

situations (which do not necessarily occur on all flights) are listed overleaf and are adapted from research conducted by S. J. Solberg in the United States. You will be asked to rate each of the items, according to the indicated ratings, in terms of how anxious or tense you would feel if you were in that situation: 1) right now; 2) after reading Chapter 4 and completing the relevant exercises in Chapters 5, 6 and 7; and 3) *after* you have finished the programme and taken a flight.

Rate the items listed before starting the exercises to establish your reactions now, by using a continuous line to join up the points to make a graph. If you have never flown, fill in the items to the best of your ability. Rate them again – where relevant – after completion of the exercises, using a broken line; and once more after your flight (this time use a dot-dash line to distinguish it from the others). Or you can simply use different coloured lines to represent each stage.

Total your scores, which represent your present cumulative anxiety ratings for the *anticipatory stages* (Questions 1–15) and for the period *during* a flight (Questions 16–60), and complete the summary scores below. When you have completed the recommended reading and exercises you can repeat the questionnaire and see to what extent your global score has reduced.

	Now	After exercises	After flight
Cumulative Scores			
Pre-flight stages (Qs 1–15)			
During flight stages (Qs 16–60)			
TOTAL			

Reactions & Ratings

	Rating
Panic, terror	4
Very anxious	3
Moderately anxious	2
Slightly anxious	1
Calm, relaxed	0

1. Seeing an aircraft illustrated in a magazine.
2. Hearing an aircraft flying overhead.
3. Looking through travel brochures.
4. Booking air tickets.
5. When the tickets arrive in the post.
6. A month before departure.
7. A week before departure.
8. The day/evening before departure.
9. Leaving home for the airport.
10. Watching aircraft take-off.
11. At check-in.
12. At security check.
13. In the departure lounge.
14. Announcement of delay in departure.
15. Your flight number is called.
16. Boarding the aircraft.
17. Seeing many other people on the aircraft.
18. Sitting next to the window.
19. Fastening your seat belt.

42

Reactions & Ratings

	Panic, terror	Very anxious	Moderately anxious	Slightly anxious	Calm, relaxed
	4	3	2	1	0

20. Closure of aircraft door and realisation you cannot leave.
21. Waiting for taxying.
22. Start up of engine.
23. Taxying to runway.
24. Demonstration of safety routines.
25. Announcement by captain of flight details.
26. Waiting for take-off.
27. Seeing heavy rain and windy conditions out of window.
28. Engines rev up.
29. Accelerating down runway and being pushed back in your seat.
30. At lift off.
31. Mechanical noises under the fuselage shortly after take-off.
32. Looking out of the window you see the ground receding.
33. Vibration of the cabin during the steady climb.
34. During the climb you feel some turbulence.
35. Hearing a cut back in engine power.
36. Banking to the left and a clear view of the ground.

Reactions & Ratings

	Panic, terror 4	Very anxious 3	Moderately anxious 2	Slightly anxious 1	Calm, relaxed 0

37. The call bell sounds and the seat belt sign goes off.
38. The stewardess makes the announcement about seat belts and smoking.
39. Looking out of the window and not being able to see anything for cloud.
40. Hearing a loud and unspecified noise.
41. On a long flight, realising you have another six hours to go.
42. Travelling at night.
43. Travelling over deep water.
44. Travelling over high mountains.
45. Eating a meal at 35,000ft.
46. The captain makes an announcement about routeing.
47. You want to go to the toilet.
48. Walking around the cabin.
49. The seat belt sign comes on and an announcement is made about imminent turbulence.

44

Reactions & Ratings				
Panic, terror	Very anxious	Moderately anxious	Slightly anxious	Calm, relaxed
4	3	2	1	0

50. You feel a jolt and the aircraft changes altitude and loose objects are thrown around.

51. The aircraft is hit by lightning.

52. Engine power is reduced and the wing flaps are lowered.

53. You start your descent and feel a blocking in your ears.

54. The seat belt sign comes on and the announcement about landing is made.

55. Hearing the lowering of the landing gear.

56. Seeing the airport approach, and the wheels touch the ground.

57. Hearing a loud roar from the engines.

58. Taxying to the terminal building.

59. Thinking about how to negotiate the airport.

60. Prior to leaving the aircraft the aisle is blocked by other passengers.

4 Symptom check list

Whenever a person becomes anxious or stressed, they will display a characteristic pattern of responses that occur in different situations and which are consistent over time. The best way to determine your own constellation of thoughts, bodily and behavioural reactions, is to consider how you react on an aircraft (or think you would, if you have never flown), then look through the list of symptoms below and rate them according to the following scale as they apply to you:

Occurrence	Rating
Never	0
Sometimes	1
Always	2

(i) *Central nervous system*

	Score Before training	After training
Worry		
Difficulty in falling asleep		
Fitful sleep		
Nightmares or unpleasant dreams		
Poor concentration		
Preoccupation about death, dying		
Fear of falling		
Feeling of unreality		
Easily distracted		
Confused		
Hyper-vigilant		
Self-conscious		
Fear of losing control		
Fear of inability to cope		
Fear of heart attack		
Fear of going crazy		
Hyper-critical		

SCORE

(ii) *Bodily reactions*
These can be classified according to the physiological system
affected:

	Score	
	Before training	After training
Respiratory:		
Shallow breathing		
Rapid breathing		
Irregular breathing		
Choking sensation		
Breathlessness		
Pressure on thorax		
Dizziness		
Faintness		
SCORE		
Cardio-vascular:		
Palpitations		
Increased blood pressure		
Decreased pulse rate		
Dizziness		
Faintness		
Chest pain		
SCORE		
Gastro-intestinal:		
Dry mouth		
Nausea		
Loss of appetite		
Stomach discomfort		
Vomiting		
Diarrhoea		
SCORE		

	Score	
	Before training	**After training**

Genito-urinary:
    Increased desire to urinate
    Increased frequency of urination

SCORE

Skin:
    Sweating
    Face pale
    Face flushed
    Tingling sensations (paraesthesia)
    Sensation of heat
    Hot or cold extremities

SCORE

Musculo-skeletal:
    Muscle tightness (tension)
    Restlessness
    Trembling
    Shakiness
    Weakness
    Fatigued all the time
    Tension headache
    Tics (spasms)
    Tremor
    Increase in 'startle' reaction
    Difficulty in speaking

SCORE

SYSTEM   **SCORE**

Central nervous system
Bodily reactions
   Respiratory
   Cardio-vascular
   Gastro-intestinal
   Genito-urinary
   Skin
   Musculo-skeletal

   GRAND TOTAL

These scores represent your present level of functioning in relation to air travel, to which comparisons can be made over the course of the training programme to prepare you for your next, and subsequent, flights. Before we move on to self-monitoring during a flight, it is useful to summarise – in the boxes below – the results of the three questionnaires. These provide a global assessment of your base-line level of functioning, and where you are now – a simple measure of how much you are moving in the right direction.

	TOTAL SCORES		
	Pre-training	Post-training	Post-flight
Anxiety in situations related to flying			
Anxiety and stages of air travel			
Symptoms check list:			
Central nervous system			
Bodily reactions			

TABLE: Global Assessment and Progress Ratings

If you have a partner or close friend there is value in asking him or her to complete the above scales in terms of how they perceive your reactions. This affords you the opportunity to discuss the extent to which others are aware of your distress when you fly; sharing a problem with a sympathetic other

49

person generally bolsters motivation and enables an independent monitoring of your reactions over time.

5. Self-monitoring during a flight

This questionnaire is to be completed during the cruise phase of your first flight after having completed your training programme.

	YES	NO
1. Did you drink alcohol or take an anti-anxiety pill before the flight?		
2. Are you actively doing your relaxation exercises?		
3. Are you practising your self-talk routines?		
4. Are you keeping your alcohol consumption to a minimum?		
5. Are you drinking lots of water/juice?		
6. Are you sitting back in your seat?		
7. Are you breathing properly?		
8. Are you looking out of the window intermittently?		
9. Do you feel in control?		
10. Are you accepting the noise/movement variations?		

And, if your flight is longer than one hour:
11. Are you prepared to walk around the plane?
12. Are you feeling bored?

The more questions you answered affirmatively, apart from the first, the better. Every time you fly repeat this questionnaire, until you can truthfully say YES to numbers 2–12, when you will have achieved a very satisfactory outcome.

Air travel anxiety and depression

In the above assessment questionnaires no mention is made of low moods or depressive episodes which sometimes do occur in a number of anxious flyers, due to feelings of hopelessness about overcoming what they feel to be an irrational reaction to an intractable problem. Expectations of failure and concomitant feelings of sadness and regret can lead to a decision not to take further trips, which of course keeps the problem alive. When there are pressures to continue to fly for work, with family or for other reasons, the key to resolving such conflict is to modify the negative thinking by adopting a cognitive restructuring approach as detailed in Chapter 6. But if the depression persists, it is sensible to consult a doctor, who may recommend medication.

Types and classification of air travel anxiety

Since only a minority of people in the Western world has ever flown abroad, the experience remains largely novel or unknown and this inevitably contributes to the mild fear of flying which is prevalent in the population at large. In short, many people simply don't know what to expect from the experience and become anxious as a result.

The principal way of classifying anxiety about flying is according to whether it is an isolated fear or part of a number of fears occurring together, such as those of heights and confined spaces, and these can range from minor complaints to severely distressing disorders. Since a phobia of flying implies *avoidance* of air travel, the implication is that this means of travel is available, in principle; but if you are never required to fly or funds are not forthcoming, it is difficult to judge impairment. It is often possible to conceal such a concern from friends and acquaintances; indeed many people are reluctant to admit to a disability they either do not need to disclose or where doing so would produce future difficulties – eg the annual family vacation or a crucial business trip, where your presence is both expected and desired.

Individuals who are phobic only of air travel are as common as those who have multiple phobias, and far outnumber those whose distress, in contrast, developed after a psychological traumatic event involving flying, like experiencing or witnessing an aircraft crash or hijacking. This is known formally as *post-traumatic stress disorder*, and will be dealt with later.

Specific phobias: uniphobics v multiphobics

Those individuals who have one specific phobia differ from persons suffering from multi-dimensional phobias in several ways; for the latter, anxiety about flying represents only one manifestation of their general fearfulness. In 1977 Diana Ronell, a New York psychologist, conducted her doctoral research on a group of fearful flyers. Her subjects included thirty-eight uniphobics and forty multiphobics and from questionnaire data she found, as she had predicted, that the latter group reported a higher level of anxiety (according to subjective ratings) and considered the symptoms they experienced in flight as more severe, as well as displaying a greater number of symptoms. The uniphobic group, on the other hand, took more responsibility for what happened to themselves. They demonstrated a greater sense of personal autonomy and a significantly greater internal *locus of control* – that is, they perceived events as happening to them as the result of *their* influence, rather than fate, chance, luck or due to circumstances beyond their control.

Uniphobics enjoyed travelling more and had flown more frequently; they sought help for their problems for 'self-oriented' not for 'other-oriented' reasons and claimed that plane-related, compared with internal reasons, triggered the start of their flying difficulties. Dr Ronell's multiphobics rated fear of panicking as their most severe symptom, followed by fear of dying, claustrophobia and difficulties in breathing; whereas the uniphobics were most distressed by a fear of dying, followed by palpitations, fear of panicking and difficulties in breathing.

Regarding the first experience of fear of flying, a quarter of all Dr Ronell's respondents stated always having been afraid; this is particularly typical of her multiphobics. In contrast, most of the uniphobics became afraid following bad weather or turbulence in the air – ie an external rather than internal event. This study highlights that the two groups, although both manifesting aspects of air travel anxiety, differ substantially. Those with more complex phobias require a therapy programme which makes provision for dealing with all the elements of their concerns.

The multiphobic then is more generally fearful, but it is the uniphobic who becomes exasperated because the problem highlights a deficiency in an otherwise successful life. He (or she) is often a high achiever, a perfectionist, an action-oriented person who has high expectations of himself. He is caught in a conflict where, say, a disbelief in the safety of *his* aircraft clashes with the value society places in this form of transportation. He is not convinced by air safety statistics or general advice about how planes fly, once he has made up his mind that it is not safe. He dislikes taking a passive role – as one must as an airline passenger – and being in close confinement of others for several hours. This situation in itself would be anxiety-provoking on the ground, which is compounded by additional worries about safely defying gravity and the weather.

Panic disorder and agoraphobia

Panic attacks – ie the sudden onset of intense apprehension, fear or terror, usually linked with feelings of impending doom – may become associated with certain situations, including being in crowds (such as in a busy department store or airport terminal building) or travelling in lifts, over bridges or on trains. The marked fear known as *agoraphobia* is one of being alone or in places where escape might be difficult or help not available in case of need. Often the disorder comes about as a result of repeated panic attacks, and this leads to anticipatory fear of having another attack and refusal or reluctance to enter any situation that is associated with these attacks.

The most common symptoms people experience during a panic attack are: difficulty in breathing, faintness or vertigo; palpitations and chest discomfort; tingling sensations; sweating; fears of going mad, dying and of losing control; and feelings of *depersonalisation* (ie temporary loss of feeling of one's own reality, which sometimes has the effect of perceiving oneself from a distance) or *derealisation* – a loss of the

53

sense of reality concerning one's surroundings that can make one feel strangely unfamiliar and distant. Although the last two phenomena occur as adaptational mechanisms to reduce unpleasant experiences, they can create a feeling of impending catastrophe as when one anxious female flyer thought she had died and was being transported to heaven.

Panic attacks occur in two to five per cent of the general population and are feared by many anxious flyers who feel vulnerable in that situation, even though only a minority experience the intense and unpleasant symptoms described above. Agoraphobia, on the other hand, is less common – only around 0.5 per cent of the population have ever experienced this condition – though the vast majority of those who suffer from it would rate flying the worst possible situation on a personal list of anxiety-provoking situations.

The most distressing aspect of panic attacks is the inability to command one's thoughts, moods and physical reactions and the feeling of becoming out of control of functions which are ordinarily under one's influence. There are associated feelings of disorientation and confusion, and thoughts that anxiety will just keep on increasing. In extreme forms, the person will feel that they are dying or going crazy, because they have no satisfactory explanation of their distressing physical symptoms. The belief that they are trapped in a threatening and dangerous situation (the aircraft, say) confirms the sense of helplessness, and catastrophising takes over when the anxiety becomes intense – eg 'I can't control the anxiety, it won't go away, so something terrible will happen to me.' What the person *thinks* will happen depends to some extent on his bodily reactions, according to US cognitive therapist Aaron Beck – for example, if he has chest pain and hyperventilates, chances are that he will think he's going to have a heart attack; if he has strange sensations (such as muscle weakness and tremor) in his limbs, he will probably believe that a stroke will occur; and if his mental functions are impaired, that he will go crazy. Faintness, on the other hand, conjures up the inevitability of unconsciousness and death, and breathing difficulties have similar associations. But when there is generalised loss of control over internal bodily sensations, the fear is that this will lead to strange or uncontrollable behaviour. These consequences never occur of course, but the panicky individual does not know that.

Most fearful flyers who experience panic attacks or worry that they will, interpret their normal physiological changes as signs of serious internal disorders, but others focus on the view they feel others might have of them. On a plane they dislike the thought of being watched or scrutinised (see the section on *social phobia* for amplification of this).

Another concern about flying where panic can occur is the *fear of fear* or *phobophobia*, where worry about becoming anxious leads to the very consequences that the person seeks to avoid. This is resolvable like any other phobic reaction.

Fatigue and stress from other sources than the flight itself – for example, time pressures or work overload, or use of alcohol and drugs – are likely to make a person more vulnerable to panic attacks; and there are numerous instances of initial attacks related to flying following a major life event, like separation from spouse or family, bereavement of someone close, or travelling abroad for the first time.

Hormone changes are yet another class of events that may trigger panic attacks. Some attacks appear to be precipitated by pregnancy or following childbirth and hysterectomy, but these need to be construed as non-specific stressors in a person with a predisposition to develop the disorder; in other words, someone in this condition can be particularly vulnerable. Many women's anxieties about flying seem to be brought on by having children, which also relates to increased general concerns about safety and a worry about who would look after their children if they died as the result of an air crash. Research suggests that the initial trigger factors do not affect the course of the condition; moreover, the perceived source of panic is rarely attributed accurately – to internal as opposed to external circumstances – making the real causes impossible to deal with.

55

Post-traumatic stress disorder
This involves the development of symptoms following a frightening incident considered outside the normal range of human experience – eg being involved in or witnessing the rare event of an aircraft or helicopter crash – where re-experiencing of the traumatic event occurs. The incident remains in the sub-conscious and is readily activated by any associated stimulus. It is the combination of the life-threatening nature of the event and a feeling of helplessness that reminds the person of his inability to cope with the situation, and keeps the problem alive.

The traumatic event can be experienced again in the form of intrusive recollections or recurrent dreams or nightmares, and the unpleasant thoughts might include experiences such as falling, crashing, dying or drowning in the ocean. Excessive bodily arousal, such as difficulty in falling asleep or hyper-alertness, may result, and if fatalities occurred in the disaster, people often feel guilt about their own survival. When the traumatic experience involved flying, subsequent exposure to flying-related situations or activities that resemble (or sym-bolise) the original event – eg a plane with particular markings, a certain type of aircraft or destination – generally leads to intensification of symptoms, which often include depression and irritability.

This disorder is extremely rare, but vicarious involvement with an aircraft accident – via the media usually – is much more common and often sensitises anxious flyers for varying periods of time afterwards. To this day some people still avoid travelling on particular kinds of aircraft because they remember that one crashed years ago.

Social phobia
The central feature here is a persistent, irrational fear of, and compelling desire to avoid, situations where the person may be exposed to the critical scrutiny and evaluation of others. Since travelling by aircraft involves doing so in close proximity to others, a number of passengers fear that they

56

might behave in such a fashion as to make themselves feel embarrassed or humiliated. In general, fear of flying for other reasons – worry about the safety of the plane, claustrophobia etc – is the principal concern, which for the social phobic has additional damaging consequences. Such reactions are extremely distressing and are recognised by the person involved as excessive and unreasonable. Attention is usually directed towards other passengers for fear that they will notice signs of anxiety – shakiness, sweating or tremor – especially apparent when eating, and a sense that one is being watched. The belief is that they have been seen violating specific social norms, conventions or expectations regarding behaviour or appearance, and this sets up a set of negative internal monologues and a vicious cycle of symptom escalation. Avoidance of air travel is the principal way people deal with such difficulties, which are extremely rare.

General anxiety disorder
This category differs from phobias in that the fears occur in a mixed group of situations where avoidance is not feasible. Distressing internal sensations are common here; they are present most of the time and lead to a fear of loss of control – perceived dangers that need attending to, rather than avoided. Such disorders are precipitated by situations involving increased demands and inadequate coping resources, and a greater awareness of the possibility of failure – for example, re-evaluation of risk-taking activities after the birth of a child, and increased pressure of a new job following promotion. They are also triggered by situations where a person feels threatened, like working hard but never able to make ends meet financially, and by stressful events that undermine confidence.

People with this kind of anxiety disorder are generally unable to relax; they have constant anxious feelings and their mind races; they have poor concentration, fear of losing control, fear of being rejected, and experience a host of bodily symptoms such as tenseness, palpitations, sweating, faintness and general weakness. Clearly, if a person is anxious chronically, this will occur during flying too which can be construed as yet another threat confirming a feeling of vulnerability. It is estimated that less than three per cent of the general population suffer from this disorder. But most people who are anxious about flying and cannot generally unwind and relax do not have symptoms of the severity described above, nor do they avoid air travel specifically.

Onset
There are basically three types of circumstances under which the fear of flying becomes noticeable and troublesome for the first time. Encountering severe weather, especially turbulence, or real or imagined mechanical failure, is the trigger many people associate with the onset of their difficulties. A second category is current awareness (usually via the media) of air crashes; but the most common is a non-specific, insidious dread. People can often feel unwell or disturbed on a flight without being able to pinpoint the precise reason.

For those who do not understand the theory of flight and the robustness of aircraft, any variation in engine noise and plane movements beyond a narrow range are likely to lead to anxiety; and those who perceive flying as dangerous will have their worst preconceived ideas about aircraft confirmed in reports of accidents. Avoidance of air travel is seen to be the only viable option. As for those whose concerns are more vague, having felt uncomfortable on a plane once can increase the likelihood of this happening next time. Anticipatory anxiety will make sure of that by bringing about the self-fulfilling prophesy on the following lines: 'I felt bad last time; what if I feel bad next time? How can I be sure I don't? I don't feel well . . .' The initial worries are usually lost over time and one is left with the factors that keep it alive, of which avoidance is the most significant.

Now the details of your concerns about flying have been specified, it is time to look at how to reduce this distress.

REDUCTION

The best way to reduce your anxiety about flying is first to assess your specific problem – ie find out where you are on the air travel anxiety spectrum. The emphasis is different for everyone, but there are some common themes as you will have seen from the previous section. Pinpointing your reactions in flight-related situations will help you find appropriate techniques so that you can learn relevant coping skills. It is the matching of specific difficulties and therapeutic techniques that is the subject of this section.

A word about theory is called for at this point to obtain an understanding of the dynamics of your flying difficulties, and the aims of therapy. If flying is perceived as a threat and you do not feel you can cope with this, then it is not surprising if you feel anxious about it. (See table below.)

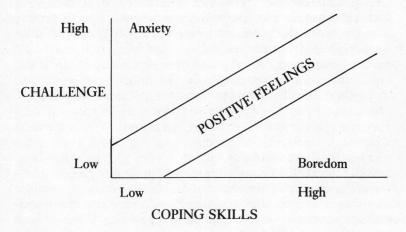

COPING SKILLS

Similarly, if you play tennis and aren't very good and you are expected to play the club champion, you will naturally feel anxious. But just think about what he feels if he has to play you – no challenge and lots of excess skill on his part. So *boredom* (and perhaps frustration in his case) is likely to be his reaction. Boredom, not enjoyment, is therefore a desirable goal of overcoming your anxiety about air travel – ie when you have all the coping skills at your fingertips, but will have nothing to do, especially on a long flight. This is why it is important to prepare yourself for eventual boredom on a flight – a sign that you are doing very well – and when the time comes to compensate for it by taking a good book, lively travelling companion, etc. (See also Appendix II on how to alleviate boredom during a flight.)

If you do not set your sights very high in tennis, or with respect to personal demands during a flight, and your coping skills are in keeping with this, then this is a satisfactory combination. In tennis, the example here is of someone who can hardly hit the ball over the net playing against an opponent of a similar standard. Such people often enjoy themselves, for their skills (or lack of them) and the challenges they set for themselves are balanced. I did not appreciate this for a long time but it now makes a lot of sense to me; it means that you don't have to be very good to enjoy something that involves coping skills. Flying is basically a passive activity and requires very little of the passenger. It is the letting go that most people find so difficult.

Another consideration concerns the presence of positive and/or negative feelings towards flying in relation to an upcoming journey by air. If you are an anxious flyer and have arranged to fly in three months' time, chances are you tell yourself that you can deal with this when the eventful day arrives; but as this draws closer, these thoughts recede into the background and are replaced by negative ones that build up to such a pitch that avoiding the flight seems the only possible course of action. (See table opposite.) Whereupon you at once feel relieved, but then guilt and self-recrimination take over.

Which is the lesser of two evils: going through with the flight and suffering for a while, or carrying around the negative thoughts about failure through not flying? Learning how to break the vicious cycle is what the remainder of this chapter and subsequent ones will explain. Remember that

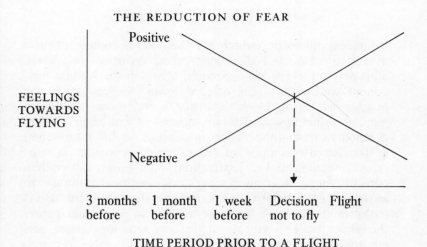

THE REDUCTION OF FEAR

FEELINGS TOWARDS FLYING

Positive

Negative

| 3 months before | 1 month before | 1 week before | Decision not to fly | Flight |

TIME PERIOD PRIOR TO A FLIGHT

TABLE: Relationship between feelings and flight avoidance

feelings follow behaviour; you have to fly to demonstrate that you can do it comfortably, rather than wait until you feel in the mood to do so.

An interesting paradox emerges. Why is it that those who believe flying is dangerous and that *their* aircraft will crash actually take flights? The main reason seems to be that when they are on the ground they know statistically that flying is safe, but the doubts about it develop and take over as the trip comes closer. They feel that their plane is the one that will go down, but on being challenged can give no detailed explanation why this should be the case. 'Rotten things always happen to me,' they say, and when they reach their destination safely, that 'Oh, I was lucky this time.' This is an example of *global labelling* and *personalisation* which will be dealt with in Chapter 6.

Principles of therapy

Therapy for anxiety about flying is not simply a matter of presenting a list of techniques. The techniques, linked to thoughts, feelings, bodily reactions and behaviour, relate to

61

strategies and tactics which are themselves rooted within a model of emotional disorders called *cognitive-behavioural*. This psychotherapeutic approach, of which the leading proponent within the areas of anxiety and depression is the psychiatrist Aaron Beck, is firmly based on a number of guiding principles, which are described below. The core component of this theoretical orientation is that the content of thinking affects a person's mood; in other words, the subjective meaning and interpretation of an event, rather than objective facts, determines a person's emotional response. In anxiety focused on particular situations, such as air travel, it is *automatic thoughts* – ie those evaluative and anticipatory thoughts that precede an unpleasant emotional state and contribute to the arousal of anxiety. Considerable research over the past ten years or so has shown that negative thinking, irrational ideas and false beliefs contribute to the generation of inappropriate or excessive anxiety (or depression). Many research investigations demonstrate the effectiveness of cognitive therapy in dealing with such problems where therapeutic strategies are derived directly from the cognitive model (see Chapter 6 for details).

In addition to the primacy of thoughts in determining mood, the essential principles of cognitive-behavioural therapy are that it is structured and directive, brief and time-limited, problem-oriented (with systematic homework essential) and presented as an educative and training process. Anxiety about air travel is explained as being due to the faulty appraisal of flying as a threat, which in turn produces changes in thoughts, feelings, bodily reactions and behaviour. It is the result of distorted, automatic thinking, and *not* the precursor to mental illness, being out of control, or death. Symptoms are the body's way of dealing with threats and danger, and behavioural responses involve either fight, flight (escape), freeze or faint, as adaptive defences.

An underlying medical condition could account for symptoms, so it is sensible to see a doctor to exclude this possibility. For example, one patient always became lightheaded and dizzy on flights whenever her eating schedule was disrupted, which made her anxious. It was not until she visited her doctor that diabetes was diagnosed, which accounted for her symptoms, and led to straightforward dietary planning for future trips. Another used to urinate several times in rapid succession prior to boarding his plane, which made him feel very uncomfortable and anxious. He explained that his practice was to drink at least six cups of coffee – a diuretic – before flights, so reducing his caffeine consumption was all that was needed to reverse his symptoms. The reason he drank so much was that he generally flew early in the day and wanted to ensure he kept awake.

Case illustrations with therapeutic strategies and tactics

In the Assessment section of this chapter, the types of anxiety that people express in relation to flying are listed. Let us now examine a case illustration from each and see what techniques (and in what combination) are appropriate and why. This will give you a flavour of the way a therapeutic programme is determined, constructed and implemented. The outcome in every case, you will be pleased to know, was successful.

Air travel anxiety and depression

Case A depressed woman in her forties was referred by her psychiatrist who was treating her with anti-depressant medication. Her husband travelled regularly all over the world in connection with his work, and they had been based abroad in the past. She was unable to join him on his travels because 'every aspect' of flying frightened her; her avoidance of flying compounded the situation. She felt hopeless and helpless and a failure as a partner.

Formulation The patient had lost hope of change and her life was devoid of rewarding activities. Her thoughts were negative and she had blocked out the specifics of flying that concerned her and labelled it as impossible to travel that way, yet at the same time considered it crucial that she could fly. Avoidance kept the problem alive.

Approach 1. Establish goals/targets regarding how she wanted to lead her life differently.
2. Relate problem to antecedents and consequences.
3. Cognitive therapy for depression.
4. Programming of activities for mastery and pleasure.
5. Anxiety management – bodily reactions and self-talk.
6. Principles of flight explained.
7. Brief flight by self.
8. Longer flight with husband.

Specific phobias
(1) *Single*
Case A successful advertising director in his thirties who had previously flown extensively suddenly developed a concern about dying in the air, related to a feeling of confinement and worry that the aircraft would not get off the runway or stay in the air. His reaction was panic exacerbated by engine noise changes and turbulence. He needed to fly for work and wanted to do so for family trips as well.

Formulation This was a man who was in control of the rest of his life. Onset of the problem was around the time his first child was born and linked to a re-evaluation of his risk-taking activities. Frustration at not being able to control the situation (and his destiny) made him feel vulnerable, compounded by the fact that he didn't understand how aircraft fly.

Approach 1. Explanation of flying as perceived threat.

2. Theory of flight and normal variations in flight.

3. Anxiety management – bodily relaxation and cognitive reappraisal.

4. Session on cockpit simulator at airport to familiarise with engine noise change and turbulence.

5. Short flight along with visit to flight deck.

(2) *Multiple*

Case A female teacher in her forties was affected by claustrophobia (lifts and trains) which made it impossible for her to contemplate flying. She wanted to travel on family holidays abroad, which had never been possible previously because of the problem.

Formulation Avoidance was keeping this lady's problem alive, for she believed that confrontation would lead to panic and becoming out of control.

Approach 1. Explanation that what follows anxiety is relaxation, nothing worse.

2. Anxiety management – bodily relaxation and cognitive restructuring.

3. Prolonged exposure to situations perceived to be claustrophobic and anxiety-provoking, coupled with use of coping strategies – ie staying in a lift long enough for anxiety to subside while being supervised and supported.

4. Short flight with walk around the aircraft.

Panic disorder and agoraphobia

Case This woman in her twenties had flown many times without problems until she was involved in a motorway accident when a car went into the back of the one she was driving. Since then she had become agitated about travelling by car, and this extended to any movement

65

beyond a few miles radius of where she lived. She felt that were she to travel by air she would panic and be in constant fear of the plane crashing.

Formulation The car accident sensitised this person to the possibility of future dangers while travelling, which generalised to busy department stores and any unfamiliar places (ie she developed agoraphobia) as the direct result of a panic attack while away from home. Avoidance of threatening situations served to maintain the status quo.

Approach 1. Discussion about panic, its determinants and consequences.
2. Anxiety management – diaphragmatic breathing, biofeedback, and self-talk routines.
3. Programme of tasks involving leaving home and travelling by car to increasingly distant places, with various activities at destination.
4. Short flight.
5. Long-haul flight.

Generalised anxiety disorder

Case A successful sales representative, who was subjected to a great deal of pressure from work and at home, developed increased anxiety symptoms when he was told about a sales conference he had to attend which involved a flight. He had a history of problems with respect to heights, cable cars, lifts and injections, and had never been able to relax and unwind completely. He was a hard-driving person who allowed himself no social life.

Formulation This man led a self-destructive lifestyle; his distress became intolerable when he could see no way of avoiding the threat of flying. He thought he was going to die because his principal symptoms were palpitations and sweating, headaches, shakiness and pins and needles, which he interpreted as signs of severe illness.

Approach 1. Explanation of symptoms and consequences of panic and avoidance.
2. Anxiety management – biofeedback for the sweating and cognitive restructuring.
3. Time management – setting up priorities and making time for relaxation and socialising with wife and others.
4. Physical exercise – he was a keen runner.
5. Short flight with friend for support.

Social phobia

Case This introverted woman in her fifties expressed anticipatory anxiety about flying in terms of worry that she would get fearful and not be able to control this. For her the consequence of this was worsened because she also concerned herself about how other passengers would react to her – ie see her as different, and judge her negatively. This made her worry about being embarrassed and vulnerable in company, and was the main reason why she had never flown. It also had a considerable effect on her social life.

Formulation This woman was anxious about air travel because of the uncertainty of what to expect. She neither understood how aircraft fly or what was expected of her as a passenger. She felt she should fly because of missing out on foreign travel to exotic places, but this produced conflict due to worry about public scrutiny both during and after the flight.

Approach 1. Principles of flight.
2. Challenging her basic assumptions regarding the views she felt others had of her.

67

3. Anxiety management – to teach relevant coping skills regarding the flight.
4. Short round-trip flight with friend.
5. Social skills training in a group.

Post-traumatic stress disorder

Case This man in his thirties was a passenger in a helicopter which crashed into the sea. He was able to leave the helicopter and was picked up by a rescue craft; there were no fatalities but the experience left him phobic of travelling by helicopters, fixed-wing planes and sailing. He had repeated nightmares and flashbacks of this traumatic episode. He needed to fly in connection with his work in the oil industry.

Formulation Although the accident took place in a helicopter, this man's phobic anxiety extended to aeroplanes and sailing, the latter because fuel smells on a boat reminded him of those of the helicopter. He had a realistic fear of travelling by helicopter and was thrown into conflict as this is the only form of transport to oil rigs in the sea where he had worked for years. Off-shore rigs provided a good source of income to which he had become dependent, and he worried about his future job potential in the light of his fear.

Approach 1. Bodily relaxation techniques relevant to his physical symptoms: muscle relaxation exercises, biofeedback, and autogenic training.
2. Cognitive therapy to put the trauma into perspective.
3. Graded exposure to sailing boats to desensitise him to fuel smells.
4. Graded exposure to relevant flying stimuli – sound tapes, video, simulator – while coping skills practised.

68

5. Brief flight in fixed-wing plane (not nearly as difficult for him as helicopter, which would probably require prolonged therapy *if* travelling, that way absolutely necessary). In any event, regular exposure to flying in aircraft until consistently relaxed, before any thought of proceeding to deal with helicopters.

Medication and alcohol

Most people who are afraid of flying do not need medication to overcome their anxiety symptoms. However, prescribed drugs which are known to reduce anxiety – called tranquillisers, anxiolytics or anti-anxiety drugs – can be very helpful when levels of discomfort are sufficiently high so as to interfere with all forms of anxiety reduction. Non-drug methods of therapy, such as breathing exercises or biofeedback, tend to be ineffective because it is impossible to focus on or attend to instructions or techniques. Talking-based therapies may be impractical in the highly anxious individual and may make symptoms worse. In other words, anxiolytic medication is used most beneficially as a temporary measure to control symptoms sufficiently for other forms of anxiety reduction to be feasible and effective. The anti-anxiety drugs of choice are, in general, the *benzodiazepines* (eg Valium and Librium) and are usually effective, given that the drug is chosen carefully and the dosage flexible, according to requirements.

Drugs reduce or at best eliminate bodily symptoms, but they cannot change the content of a person's thoughts; so that if you are worried that the aircraft will crash, removal of somatic symptoms by taking medication will not affect your feeling of flying as a threat. This is why attention needs to be paid at the same time to *cognitive restructuring* (see Chapter 6).

All anxiolytic medication requires a prescription and supervision by a doctor, who will select the most appropriate drug, monitor possible side effects and minimise dependency (which used to be much more problematic with the barbiturates that the benzodiazepines superceded, and for this reason are virtually no longer prescribed for anxiety problems). For those whose anxiety is specifically focused on something specific like flying ('state' anxiety), as opposed to having an enduring personality predisposition ('trait' anxiety), short-acting benzodiazepines such as diazepam (Valium) and lorezepam (Ativan) are preferable. The drug needs to be taken thirty minutes prior to entering the anxiety-provoking situation, and even if a panic attack has started, the medication can still be taken and will exert a fairly prompt action in terminating the panicky feelings.

For those who are more generally anxious, where anxiety increases against a background of a raised anxiety level, a proportion of the daily dose can be taken for hypnotic purposes – ie prior to bed to prevent insomnia. The drug needs to be short-acting so that sedation on the day of the flight is minimised. It is much better to have a clear head when flying so that coping strategies can be put into practice. Avoid taking more than the prescribed dose of anxiolytics; if you do exceed the dose, then prepare for common unwanted side effects, including tiredness, drowsiness, apathy and sluggishness, which occur within two hours of ingestion of the tablets – possibly in the middle of a flight, making it even more difficult to cope. This is despite some reports from some people that large doses of anxiolytics and alcohol do not touch them at all, perhaps because of overriding worry regarding their personal safety on a plane.

Alcohol must not be consumed when taking benzodiazepines, for as with most drugs which have a depressant action, the effects of alcohol can be significantly increased. It can, for example, impair driving ability profoundly, even though the anti-anxiety drug may have been taken over days, weeks or months, so caution on the way to the airport must be exercised. Remember too that alcohol itself has more pronounced intoxicating effects at altitude and also increases the rate of dehydration. Try then to keep your alcohol intake to a minimum on a flight.

Both alcohol and benzodiazepines can produce uncharacteristic aggressive and hostile behaviour and excessive emotional responsiveness, such as weeping or uncontrollable giggling. This can confuse patients who, naturally, fail to attribute the symptoms to the drug or alcohol they have taken. Moreover, benzodiazepines can produce a lowering of respiratory function especially in those with respiratory conditions, such as chronic bronchitis and emphysema. Light-headedness and faintness are likely to occur due to hypoxia as a result of a build-up of carbon dioxide in the bloodstream. This is because the drug makes the part of the brain that controls respiration less sensitive to arterial carbon dioxide.

For those with predominant complaints which include the following physical symptoms – palpitations, tremor, stomach upset or diarrhoea, without impairment of mental functioning – there are drugs which exert action on the part of the autonomic nervous system (the beta division of the sympathetic branch) which are very effective in reducing such symptoms. The drugs are called beta-blockers (more formally known as *beta-adrenoceptor antagonists*), the best example of which is propanolol (trade name: Inderal). Somatic symptoms, such as headache, or general psychological symptoms are not affected by these drugs due to different neurophysiological mediators, and are therefore not warranted in this situation. Furthermore, beta-blockers should not be used with anyone with a history of asthma, and specialist advice needs to be taken for those with heart disease.

It must be stressed, however, that improvement due to beta-blockers may well be limited to the symptoms described above; other anxiety symptoms are likely to be unchanged. A number of anxious flyers use their physical symptoms, such as palpitations, to signal their closeness to a flight, which ordinarily leads to avoidance. When these sensations are eliminated by beta-blockers, the flight may be taken, which unwittingly exposes them to the phobic situation. This is why a full assessment and treatment programme is needed prior to travelling so that such problems can be prevented.

Where depression is the primary complaint, where there is anxiety and agitation, several anti-depressants of the *tricyclic* variety, such as amitriptyline, doxepin and mianserin, possess beneficial secondary sedative properties, but like all the above drugs, they are available only on prescription. If those people who have been taking anti-anxiety medication do not respond to this treatment it is possible that there is an underlying problem of depression which needs to be evaluated. If necessary, a doctor can refer on to a psychiatrist for expert assessment of this.

The key issue regarding the use of anti-anxiety drugs for the anxious flyer is whether these are recommended simply for expediency as a simple device to suppress symptoms without consideration of cognitive factors, rather than because the anxiety is so severe that it *interferes* with ability to cope with the acute distress and underlying problems. There is a danger of 'medicalising' what is basically a defensive response to the perceived environmental (and maybe inter-personal) threat of flying. It is important to remember that most acute anxiety states subside spontaneously (as indicated in Table A) and as a function of repeated exposure (as shown in Table B), though a few become long-lasting if the symptoms are allowed to persist.

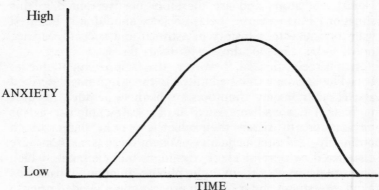

TABLE A: Course of anxiety over time

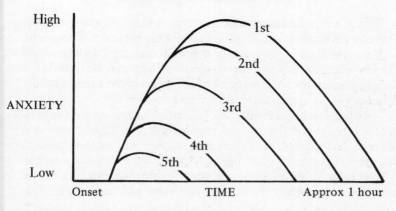

TABLE B: Anxiety as function of repeated exposure to fearful stimuli over time

It is advisable to raise these points with your doctor if he or she recommends anti-anxiety medication.

Prevention

This chapter explains what can be done to help those who are anxious about flying. But how does one ensure that such problems do not develop in the first place? Several clients have expressed concern that they do not want their children to become anxious about flying like they are. Much learning of behaviour takes place as a result of seeing significant people in one's life – parents, teachers, friends – react in similar situations, and so behaving positively in such situations is of paramount importance. This needs to be complemented by an explanation of the facts about flying, for ignorance is definitely undesirable, along with appropriate emotional regard to such information – ie although reading about an aircraft accident can be an emotional experience, this has to be put into proper perspective. Explaining about the variations in flight, noises and movements, as changes along a broad continuum of normal functioning, will reinforce appropriate expectations for future flights.

73

The airline industry can contribute through realistic television commercials and balanced documentaries. Those who dominate commercial aviation find flying a pleasurable and even exciting experience – views which are reflected, for example, in advertisements, choice of in-flight films, and the behaviour of flight and cabin crews.

Airlines are becoming increasingly aware of passengers' concerns about flying, and the training of flight and cabin crews has started to reflect this. Awareness of, and how to cope with, fearful passengers, discouraging excessive use of alcohol and developing pleasing cabin interiors and seat designs to promote relaxation and minimise anxiety, all help in this respect; along with explanatory announcements, especially when circumstances occur which are out of the ordinary, such as a particularly hard landing. There is no evidence that the non-anxious passenger responds with anxiety to such developments, though the frequent flyer values minimum distractions so he or she can sleep, work or whatever.

Matching symptoms and techniques

It is most useful to divide symptoms into three categories: knowledge about flying, bodily symptoms and cognitive concerns – all of which require different kinds of techniques, which are summarised in the table opposite. A tick indicates that you should definitely read that chapter.

You are now recommended to proceed to Chapters 4, 5 or 6, and in that order learn more about the techniques that will help you. The probability is that you will find some benefit from reading all of these, and it would be most logical to go through them in sequence. Chapters 7, 8 and 9 add further refinements once you have learned basic coping skills. Do not forget to monitor your progress with the exercises by repeating the evaluation questionnaires in the Assessment section of this chapter, and again once you have flown.

	Theory of flight (Ch 4)	Bodily relaxation (Ch 5)	Defusing worrying thoughts (Ch 6)
No or little knowledge about how planes fly	✓		
Bodily symptoms		✓	
Irrational ideas and negative thoughts about flying			✓

TABLE: Matching Symptoms and Techniques

4
Principles of Flight

We by skill gain mastery over things
in which we are conquered by nature.
ANTIPHON

Brief history of aviation
Man's desire to emulate nature is evident in the works of art
of the earliest civilisations and in the traditions of many
peoples. One of the first accounts of an attempt to fly is that
relating to the Chinese Emperor Shun of the third millen-
nium BC who made his escape from captivity by donning the
'work-clothes of a bird'. An eleventh-century Anglo-Saxon
monk named Eilmer is credited as one of the first airmen. He
fastened wings to his hands and feet, and collecting the
breeze across the summit of a tower, managed to fly for over
250 yards. He broke both his legs on landing – a better fate
than for the many others over the centuries who fell to their
deaths trying to emulate Icarus.

It was not until the fifteenth century that serious attention
was paid to the possibility of developing an effective
mechanical aeronautical device. Leonardo da Vinci, who
studied bird flight, speculated upon the mechanism behind
this ability, and designed a flapping wing structure in which a
man cranked a winch to simulate bird-like motion. But such
experimentation was rare and this delayed progress considerably. In fact, a major breakthrough was not achieved for over
three hundred years, when in 1804 Sir George Cayley, a
Yorkshire baronet, pointed to the importance of fixed

cambered or curved wings rather than the existing flappers; but it was not until 1853 that he tested the world's first successful flying machine. He developed a glider that flew over short distances with passengers aboard – and also, incidently, invented the caterpillar tractor.

However, the era of sustained powered flight did not begin until this century, when the famous Wright brothers built and piloted a 750lb biplane on a 12 second, 120 foot inaugural flight, followed on the same day by another flight 59 seconds long, covering a distance of half a mile. This momentous occasion took place on 17 December 1903, and it introduced the world's first genuinely successful heavier-than-air flying machine. Within two years the Wright brothers' 1903 flyer had been transformed into a practical aircraft capable of manoeuvring (ie turning, banking, etc) with complete freedom under the pilot's control.

The world's first commercial airline service was started in 1914 in the USA, and this was followed in 1919 by the world's first international scheduled airline service (between London and Paris). Most of the flying after World War I focused on carrying mail, but the occasional passenger was begrudgingly transported. By the late 1920s, converted fighter planes were replaced by purpose-built airliners which were extremely luxurious, and in 1930 the first air stewardesses were introduced, all of whom were trained nurses. In the thirties all-metal aircraft made their appearance, as did sleeping booths on them for overnight travel. (These have now been selectively re-introduced by a number of airlines to woo first-class travellers.) The trend for opulence was shortlived due to the outbreak of World War II, but this had its benefits in the laying down of new runways worldwide and in the acceleration of research, the principal result of which was the invention of the jet engine. This led in the 1960s to the development of wide-bodied jet-liners, supersonic aircraft and enormous turbofan engines offering increased power, reduced noise and better fuel efficiency, which in turn led to a dramatic expansion in commercial jet aviation.

The Boeing 707 arrived in 1958, a year after the Hawker Siddeley Trident (the first rear-engined 'tri-jet'), and became the world's most successful jet transport (sales of 1,500 and in service with eighty-five airlines by 1978). The first wide-bodied jet, the Boeing 747, made its maiden flight in 1969; it could carry up to 550 passengers. The largest Western aircraft in operation, however, is the American C-5A Galaxy, a military cargo aircraft; it is eighty-three yards long and can hold up to six single-decker (Greyhound) coaches. It is also used to airlift mobile hospitals to worldwide disaster areas and for carrying limousines and security vehicles for American presidential travels. The Russians have since built a larger plane.

The fastest commercial aircraft is the supersonic Anglo-French Concorde, which made its inaugural flight with British Airways and Air France in 1976. Its cruising speed is twice the speed of sound (1,340mph) at an altitude of 55,000–60,000ft – over ten miles high. In 1980 it took only 2 hours, 59 minutes and 14 seconds to fly from New York's Kennedy Airport to London Heathrow. (The absolute world air speed record, established by the US military Lockheed SR-71A in 1976, stands at 2,193mph.) Unfortunately, the long-term future of Concorde as a commercially viable operation may be in doubt in view of its high noise levels and massive fuel costs.

The 'miracle' of flight

It seems remarkable that so much has happened in aviation in such a short space of time; after all, there are many people still alive who were born before man flew in the first powered aeroplane. Today one billion people travel by air every year, but many of them do not understand the 'miracle' of flight. For the anxious flier, knowledge of this kind is often not enough to resolve the problem; but removing the uncertainty and misconceptions about how such a large object leaves the ground and stays in the air, what engine-noise changes and other sounds mean, and how the pilot avoids other planes can be extremely reassuring. Not to mention having the answers to questions such as: why doesn't the wing fall off as it bends so much? what if the engines stop? how can the pilot find his way in poor visibility? isn't bumpiness dangerous?

How then does a plane such as a Boeing 747 Jumbo, which is made mostly of metal (with a wing span of nearly 200ft, longer than the distance covered by the Wright brothers' first powered flight) and can weigh over 370 tons when fully loaded, get off the ground, fly not far below the speed of sound at an altitude of around 40,000ft, and stay in the sky for up to half a day? This is how.

Only four components are absolutely necessary for an aircraft to do its job: wings for flight, a tail for stability, movable exterior surfaces for control, and some source of power to provide the thrust. Everything else is peripheral – somewhere to sit, radar, toilets . . . The relationship of the four components is crucial and this is the reason why the development of the aeroplane took a long time to reach fruition. Several crucial breakthroughs punctuated this slow progress, the first of which was related to the invention of gliders, powerless kite-like objects with fixed wings. For centuries, the prevailing view was that in order to build an effective flying machine the wings had to move in a bird-like fashion. The second breakthrough involved the application of a two hundred-year-old rule from physics called Bernouilli's theorem, after the Belgian mathematician and physicist of the same name, which states that a gas loses internal pressure as it moves at high speeds. And when a gas loses internal pressure it weighs less. How does this apply to flying?

Lift
Air is a gas and the wings of a plane move through air in the same way that a fish moves through water. The top surface of a wing is curved convexly so that air passing over it has to travel farther than if the surface were straight – just as you have to travel a longer distance to get to Amsterdam from Paris if you visit London along the way.

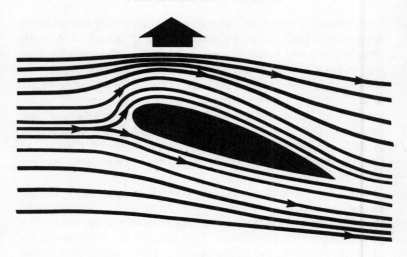

Lift and airflow. The flow of air above an aircraft wing is constricted and therefore speeds up. This produces low pressure, so the higher pressure below it actually *pushes* the wing up towards the lower pressure. As a result, the plane rises.

In order to travel the extra distance produced by the wing's curve, air has to move more quickly. So in terms of Bernouilli's theorem, the air over the wing loses pressure and weight as it moves faster. The heavier air below therefore pushes the wing into the lighter air; in other words, the wing rises, and so does the rest of the aircraft with it.

Exactly the same principle applies in sailing: air passes over the convex side of a boat's sail and as a result the boat is literally pulled along rather than pushed – this explains why boats need to tack *into* the wind for forward movement (although of course they can run with the wind too), and resolves the confusion many people have about this and other seemingly incongruous sailing manoeuvres.

The necessary ingredient for lift to take place is a curved wing *moving through air*. Movement alone is not enough – although some fast motor cars, for example, need spoilers (a wing-like structure but with a concave curved surface) over the rear wheels in order to keep them on the ground at speed!

A useful demonstration of lift is to put your arm out of your car window when travelling along the road as if you were about to make a right turn (or left hand turn if you drive on the right). Keep your hand open with your palm parallel to the ground and your fingers pointing out. You will find that your hand seems to be supported on the air and no effort is required to keep it there. Now tilt the edge of your hand upward – with your thumb higher than your little finger – and notice that your hand will tend to rise. As you increase the speed of the car, lift forces increase in strength. Just imagine that force multiplied many thousand times, and you have the situation in an aircraft.

Another little test of the lift principle is to make an airfoil out of paper. This helps to dispel notions held by many that an aircraft can (and might well) 'fall like a stone' out of the sky.

First of all, fold an A4 or foolscap size of paper in half, width wise – being careful *not* to flatten the folded edge. Hold that edge about six inches in front of you at the level of your mouth, and blow in the direction of the fold. Chances are that nothing will occur apart from non-specific fluttering of the paper. If, however, you position the top edge about a quarter of an inch away from the bottom one, and repeat the exercise, you will find that the paper will lift, according to Bernouilli's theorem. You have, in practice, created an airfoil, due to the raised curve on the top surface. This aerodynamic model will lift so long as there is sufficient air speed over it (see the later section on power for details of this). The harder you blow on the fold, the greater the lift will be produced.

Another way of demonstrating the lift phenomenon is to hold the two shorter corners of an A4 or foolscap sheet of paper between your fingers and in front of your mouth, letting the paper hang loose. Blow strongly *over* the top surface of the paper and you will see that the entire sheet lifts – just like the wings of an aircraft.

If an aircraft is light and has a large wing-surface area, relatively little power will be required to make it fly, as it will be able to do so at a slower speed than a heavy plane with small wings (such as a wide-bodied Boeing 747). The Jumbo and similar aircraft need much more power to fly, and the airflow over the wings must be maintained at a much greater speed in order for the plane to stay in the air.

Stability

Fixed wings by themselves have little stability and are unable to stay in the air for long without another appendage: the tail. This is the reason why an arrow requires a tail to reach its target, and the same goes for a simple kite or model aircraft. Otherwise, the wings would move in unwanted ways due to the various (and unwanted) forces acting upon them.

Whereas a train has only one freedom of motion (forward or backward), and a car two (it can also turn left or right), an aircraft has three: in addition to the other movements, it can climb or descend. Furthermore, the aircraft is able to move in other ways within these three basic freedoms of motion: it can pitch nose-up or down, or both, along its lateral axis (wingtip to wingtip); it can roll along its longitudinal axis (nose to tail); and the nose can move from left to right and back again about its vertical axis – this movement is known as yawing. In order to correct for yawing, the tail assembly of an aircraft (technically referred to as the empennage) possesses an upright fin; its most prominent feature. This enables the aircraft to resist unwanted sideways movement, and is called the vertical stabiliser. To control for pitch, horizontal structures protrude from both sides of the vertical fin or tailplane to balance the aircraft on its wings; these are the horizontal stabilisers.

Every aircraft uses a variety of movable surfaces to achieve control over each of the above axes. Elevators on the tailplane control pitch by moving up and down: when they move up the aircraft climbs and when down the plane loses altitude. The rudder, along with the ailerons, helps to prevent yawing and steer the plane – when the rudder is left and the left wing is

Aircraft and movement. A train can move only forward and back, a car in addition left and right, but a plane can also climb or descend. Within each of these axes of motion an aircraft is able to: a) move left or right about its vertical axis – known as *yawing* (top); b) move laterally nose-up or down about an imaginary line from wing-tip to wing-tip – known as *pitching* (middle); and c) move longitudinally about a line from nose to tail – known as *rolling* (bottom). These are all normal movements and occur on every flight.

down, the plane moves to the left. The ailerons, by moving in opposite directions, enable the plane to make smooth turns by banking the wings; this is the same principle by which bicycles and motorbikes take bends. Lift is lost on the side where the aileron is raised, but it is gained on the side where the lowered aileron increases the curve of the wing. The function of the ailerons is improved by spoilers positioned on the top surface of wings, which when raised result in the wing on that side dropping. When both spoilers are raised overall lift falls, drag rises and the plane slows down and descends. After landing they serve to 'spoil' the lift produced by the wings and make sure the plane stops on the ground. Wing flaps help to lift the plane on take-off; they move backward

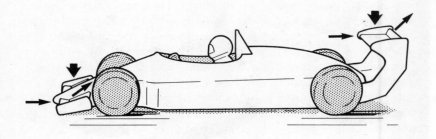

Stability and speed. Racing and other high performance cars which are aerodynamic – like planes – have *dams* at the front and *spoilers* at the back that transmit forces onto their fat tyres, which make them more stable at speed. Otherwise, they too would take-off – just like aircraft.

and down and on landing assist the slowing down process. Slats assist the function of the flaps – by moving forward and down in front of the wing on take-off and landing, they enable the aircraft to achieve more lift at slower speeds.

Power

This is the fourth crucial ingredient which enables an aircraft to function as an aircraft. The principle behind the workings of an aircraft engine can be best explained by another rule of physics; this time Isaac Newton's third law, which states that action and reaction are equal and opposite. When applied to flying this means that the action of an engine in pushing air backward produces a reaction by which the engine and plane to which it is attached are literally pushed forward. Practical demonstrations you can conduct to illustrate this reaction include releasing the air from a balloon – when you let go of it, the balloon will move in the opposite direction to the air that escapes. And in pushing against a wall, you push your body *away* from the wall. Also, watch the next rocket launch from Cape Kennedy: you will see engine flames going in the opposite direction to the movement of the rocket.

Until the early 1940s propellers – simply rotating wings –

attached to large and powerful petrol-driven, internal-combustion piston engines (similar to car engines but with more cylinders) provided the necessary air speed for the wings to create lift. The propeller itself pulls the aircraft forward; at the same time the blades channel the air backwards converting lift into propulsive thrust, the level of which is directly proportional to the speed of the propeller. In the forties, aircraft propulsion was revolutionised by the development of the jet engine – the inspiration of Frank Whittle, who had the basic idea when he was a twenty-two-year-old pilot officer in the R.A.F. more than a decade before. The first passenger plane to incorporate jet engines was the British Comet in 1949.

Jet propulsion can be explained as a propelling force that moves an aircraft forward in reaction to the momentum of gases accelerating out of the rear of the engine. The jet engine consists essentially of three sections: compressor, combustion chamber, and turbine. Air is taken in through the front of the engine and is compressed by the compressor, which consists of a series of fan blades similar to propellers; these rotate at speed. This high-pressure air is then mixed with a kerosene-like fuel (a low-grade paraffin equivalent to that used in domestic heating stoves) in the combustion chamber and passes through a second series of fans – the turbines – before leaving hot and at high-velocity through the exhaust pipe at the rear of the plane. The high energy air in passing over the turbine runs the compressor, which keeps air flowing into the engine. This process of speeding up the air through the engine produces internal forces that push the aircraft forward at high speeds by generating thousands of pounds of thrust. Each of the four Rolls-Royce RB211 engines, for example, which provide the power for some of the newer Boeing 747s, develops over 50,000lb of thrust – sufficient energy to service a town with a population of 100,000. The advantages of the jet engine over its predecessor – the propeller-driven engine – are that it produces far more power (weight for weight) and is considerably more efficient at high altitude and high speed; it has fewer moving parts and is easier to maintain, is more reliable and allows for more streamlining, thereby reducing drag. And importantly, all jet aircraft are designed to fly and land safely on only one engine, regardless of how many they actually possess.

The principles of flight in summary

The engines push air towards the rear of the plane and the aircraft is pushed forward (according to Newton's third law). As a result of this movement air passes over the wings; the component which passes over the top of the wing produces a drop in air pressure, and lift is created (Bernouilli's theorem). At a particular threshold, which varies according to the gross weight of the plane and weather conditions etc, the aircraft leaves the ground. When this occurs the tail assembly provides stability and the other movable surfaces provide all the necessary control.

Phases of a flight

For many commercial aircraft passengers, especially fearful ones, flights seem to just happen. Because of poor information, wrong information or overriding emotional reasons, they do not appreciate that for every flight there is a logical and ordered sequence of stages (taxying through cruise to landing), and a series of fully explainable changes, the most relevant of which for the traveller are engine and other mechanical noises, aircraft movements and turbulence.

The distinct phases of a flight are:

Parked

This is when the aircraft is stationary at, or close to, a terminal and occurs before or after taxying. Most commonly these days passengers are boarded directly from the terminal building via a covered gangway called a 'finger', but if the plane is parked some distance away, transport is provided and boarding takes place using passenger steps; these adapt telescopically to any aircraft door height. Some airports, like

Dulles International in Washington DC, employ mobile lounges which reduce apron congestion by transporting passengers to a parked aircraft away from the terminal. The cabin scissor-lifts to connect with any aircraft door or terminal gate. They can carry up to 150 passengers and cushion their occupants from the weather outside.

Taxi

Taxying commences when the aircraft moves from its parked position, with specially designed tugs (using an attachment to the nosewheel) pushing it backwards from the parking bay, and continues up to the start of the take-off run. On completion of the landing run at the end of a flight, the plane then taxis to the terminal gate, or point when the engines are stopped. The pilot steers the aircraft on the ground by using a small steering wheel which is located to the left of the captain's seat. This is often the bumpiest part of the whole trip!

Take-off

Take-off refers to the period from commencement of the take-off run until the wheels leave the ground (known technically as 'unstick').

How then can such an enormous object as an aircraft get off the ground and stay in the air? We have seen how lift produced by the wings and thrust generated by the engines are the positive forces which enable the plane to take off and keep in the air, but there are two others that act against these: drag (caused by the resistance of the air against the plane's shape) and weight of the aircraft. Lift derived from the airflow over the wings overcomes weight, and thrust from the engines more than compensates for the drag factor. So long as lift and thrust are equal to or more than drag and weight, the plane, whether a single-engined, two-seater private aircraft or a commercial 400-seater wide-bodied jet, will be able to fly and remain in the air. The same is true of helicopters, where a rotor replaces the fixed wing to produce lift.

The actual weight of the aircraft determines the speed necessary for take-off. Obviously the more weight the wings have to lift, the faster the plane has to travel down the runway (speed is also a function of wing design), but maximum take-off weights are specified for all types of aircraft. At airports where temperature or altitude is high, greater speeds are needed for take-off to occur; this is because the air is rarefied and, as you now know, air density is relevant to the process of lift. Runways at major airports are often two to three miles long – those in hot climates or at high altitudes need to be longer than those at ground level – distances which are necessary to achieve the required speeds prior to take-off. This can take close to one minute from the start.

As lift is dependent upon air speed it is preferable for aircraft to take-off into wind, for this enables the plane to get off the ground at a slower speed, thereby saving expensive fuel. However, this is not always possible; strict criteria are laid down as to what to do where, say, the prevailing wind is a crosswind (in this case there are often other runways available which minimise the impact of this).

Prior to departure, a decision is made by the flight crew regarding minimum take-off speed for that particular flight; this is known as 'velocity one' (V_1) and is based on the assumption that an engine will fail during this critical period – ie a built-in assurance that ample power will still be available given such a rare contingency. But even if it did happen – more than a million to one chance against – the plane would still be able to climb away and land safely. Up to V_1 speed lift-off can be aborted, were an engine to fail, by the application of wheel brakes, spoilers and reverse thrust.

When an aircraft approaches the minimum speed for take-off, at a speed known as 'velocity-rotate' (V_R), also determined prior to the flight, its nose is raised off the ground to about twelve degrees from the horizontal – a process called 'rotation'. This leads to greater lift as the 'angle of attack' (the angle at which the aerofoil meets the flow of air) increases, and overcomes the aircraft's weight. (Rotation produces in

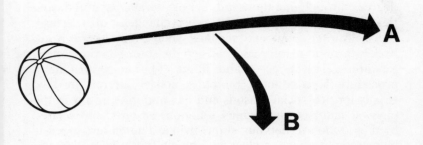

Velocity and direction. When a ball is thrown with sufficient force, the trajectory is similar to the path shown in A. It is impossible for it to fall to the earth as in B. Exactly the same principle applies to aircraft.

many anxious fliers a sensation of falling, but this is simply due to sudden excitation of the organ of balance located in the inner ear, and can be neutralised to a great extent if a deep breath is taken at the time of take-off.)

Initial climb
This covers the period from leaving the ground to 1,500ft, or until the flaps etc are retracted, whichever is higher. Within a minute of take-off the undercarriage is rehoused and the aircraft is set to climb at 'velocity two' (V_2), the speed calculated to produce the best angle of climb for the weight. This angle is usually 15–20 degrees, though it often seems much more to the anxious traveller. However, should a relatively steep climb or turn from the airport be necessary – as in Nice or with some runways at Kennedy Airport in New York – to avoid high-level terrain or built-up areas for noise abatement reasons, then a lower weight capacity is indicated.

Climb
After the initial stage the aircraft continues to climb until it reaches the first en route altitude (top of climb or cruise level). At this time the angle of the aircraft is around 3–5

degrees through one thousand feet or therabouts; and during this phase of the flight engine-noise changes can be heard, especially after about sixty seconds when engine power is cut back by around ten per cent to keep the sound on the ground to within relatively acceptable limits. This noise abatement procedure is conducted on older/noisier aircraft by law, strictly for pro-social reasons and has nothing to do with the physical status of the engines, a notion not often appreciated by those who are nervous about flying. Thereafter, speed is increased – subject to clearance by air traffic control – and the flaps are retracted to bring the plane into a cruise configuration. Throughout the flight the angle of climb is kept to less than twenty degrees, as at some critical point beyond this the airflow over the wing surface would become turbulent and lift would be lost, a condition known as wing 'stall'; this is least likely to occur when the angle of climb is shallow.

Cruise
From top of climb to top of descent, including any en route climb or descent, the aircraft is cruising. Many passengers assume that once this part of the flight is reached any deviation from the cruise altitude must mean that there is a problem. There are two main reasons for changing altitude during a cruise: first to avoid or minimise turbulent weather conditions (less likely at high altitude anyway); second to save money, since it is more economical to fly higher as the plane's fuel – which comprises a significant proportion of its weight – is burned off.

Both the cruising speed and the range of the aircraft (ie the distance it can remain in the air) depend on the power output of the engine: more power leads to more thrust, hence higher speed, but higher fuel consumption lowers the effective range. Most aircraft cruise at fifty-five per cent power – the lower end of cruise power. This is known as the 'economy power setting' and is generally adopted by all commercial airlines due to the extremely high cost of fuel. As jet engines function more efficiently and economically at high compared to low altitude, the higher an aircraft flies the further it can travel on the same amount of fuel.

Many fearful passengers worry about flying at high level and forget that the higher the altitude the longer an aircraft will take to return to earth, thus providing additional time for action if there is any problem. Although large commercial jets do not make good gliders, they do have a range of about 175 miles or half an hour should all the power be shut off at cruise altitude. This happened in 1983 to a British Airways' flight over Java after the engines ingested volcanic dust; the plane lost considerable altitude but the engines reignited at 12,000ft, and the journey concluded uneventfully.

Descent

This is from top of the descent to arrival over the outer marker (1,500ft) above an airport on final approach. If power produced by the engines is below what is required at a particular air speed, then a negative rate of climb or 'rate-of-sink' results. Like the rate of climb, the rate of descent is *fully* controllable.

On a long-distance flight, descent starts more than one hundred miles from the airport. In order to produce extra lift at slower speeds, the wing flaps are extended. This produces whirring and grinding noises which can be noticed inter-mittently. During this phase air speed changes are minimal; the aircraft will probably bank as it is brought into line with the airport traffic pattern, which is organised by air traffic controllers at the airport and elsewhere.

Holding

This involves flying a set procedure at a predetermined point which deliberately delays an aircraft landing at an airport, usually because of density of traffic or bad weather. It there-fore does not occur on all flights. An aircraft is directed by Air Traffic Control to the 'hold' or 'stack', which is a designated area of air space within an airport's control zone. Each waiting aircraft flies a special circuit separated vertically from other planes by a minimum of 1,000ft. An aircraft proceeds to the next level as soon as it is free of other traffic, until it eventually leaves the stack for final landing approach.

Approach

This penultimate stage commences from the outer marker, which is a radio beacon about five miles from the airport and 1,500–3,000ft above it, to crossing the runway threshold. The aircraft's approach speed is determined by the manufacturers according to rules laid down by the relevant government authority (as all such parameters are), including a minimum speed for final approach under ideal conditions. This is known as 'V_{ref}' for which landing performance data is calculated. The heavier the aircraft, the greater the V_{ref} and the more distance needed to stop. Required runway length is determined by measuring the distance from the point at which the aircraft is fifty feet above the ground to its stopping position, for various gross weights, and then this figure is multiplied, for safety reasons, by one and two-thirds. This distance may need to be increased on wet and slippery surfaces, and landing weight has to be limited accordingly.

Aircraft approaching touchdown follow a shallow gradient; pilots use the Instrument Landing System (ILS), the standard landing aid, which assists them to land automatically in poor visibility. It is a radio system which transmits two beams: the *localiser* and *glide* path. The localiser beam (on the Very High Frequency waveband) defines the centre line of the runway and extends along the approach path for about twenty miles; whereas the glide path beam (on the Ultra High Frequency waveband) defines the angle at which the aircraft needs to fly, so that it safely clears all obstacles. The ILS can be used by suitably equipped aircraft for automatic landings. All TriStars and Boeing 747s, 757s, 767s and Airbuses have such equipment fitted as standard.

The more steeply an aircraft descends the less is the noise disturbance on the ground, but early extension of the flaps produces high drag and therefore higher fuel consumption and an increase in noise level for those on board. During final approach the landing-gear is lowered and the flaps are extended fully to slow the aircraft while maintaining lift. (You may see gaps appear between the flaps and the mainframe of the wing – don't panic, this is normal.) Both procedures have associated noise changes; at lower altitudes, as there are more gusty air currents, the ride can seem somewhat bumpy compared to the cruise phase.

Landing
Crossing the runway threshold to the end of the landing run. This final leg of the flight can be thought of as the take-off process in reverse. At the point of crossing the runway threshold the pilot lifts the nose to reduce the rate of descent and gently throttles back. Modern jets are designed to land on their wing wheels, and then tilt forward onto the front wheels. Often it is possible to detect a slight bounce as the wheels make initial contact with the ground. When the nose wheels touch down 'reverse thrust buckets' can be seen at the rear of some engines; these are used to slow down the aircraft after touchdown. They remain open throughout the flight; when they are closed exhaust fumes are deflected forward and outward, creating a backward thrust that helps the wheel brakes to lower the landing speed. (Wheel brakes become overheated if they are used alone to slow an aircraft, and are therefore only employed in this way in an emergency.)

Visual instruments called Precision Approach Path Indicators (PAPI) and Visual Approach Slope Indicators (VASI) are used to give the pilot feedback about the accuracy of his approach. These consist of high-intensity light boxes or lamps placed alongside the runway. The boxes contain red and white lights which by their configuration tell the pilot whether he is above, below or on the correct glide path.

Engine noises explained
From the above, it can be seen that the engine note changes for specific reasons at specific times – in the same way as does

93

the engine in your car. When you put your foot down on the accelerator this produces an increase in noise level (even if you are driving a Rolls-Royce!), while lifting your foot off the pedal has the opposite effect. If you require more power going up an incline, you press the pedal down. It's basically the same in an aircraft. Just remember that it is necessary to get used to these rather than expect them not to occur.

Non-engine noises explained

In addition to engine noise variations during a flight, there are other sounds about which the fearful flier needs to be aware, the most significant of which are related to the aircraft's *utility systems*. These systems make the pilot's job much easier, ease the load on the airframe, facilitate safe flight through bad weather and enable numerous operations to take place. They can be broadly equated with various systems in the human body – nervous, respiratory, digestive – and include the following: flight control, electrical, avionics (aviation electronics), hydraulic, fuel, emergency, pneumatic (air conditioning), oxygen, de-icing and anti-icing.

They are a necessary part of safe flying and without them most aircraft would be helpless. The electrical and electronic systems are relatively unintrusive from the passenger's point of view; and of the non-electronic systems, the hydraulic and air-conditioning are probably the noisiest. They involve various whining and other sounds and tend to disturb many people who do not understand why they occur or change, and think mistakenly that they mean problems.

The hydraulics, the 'muscles' of the modern aircraft, consists of up to four separate systems for safety reasons (only one of which is used at any one time) and is the method used to transfer power from one place to another through the use of a non-inflammable fluid, usually phosphate-esters. Many mechanical devices on an aircraft are operated in this way, including wing flap extension, landing gear operation, and braking with automatic anti-skid systems to ensure maximum stopping efficiency on slippery runways without allowing the

94

wheels to lock. Further hydraulics drive the nosewheel steering when the aircraft is taxying and also operate the gear mechanism in loading heavy freight. All of these have their associated noises (see Chapter 8 for details of how they can be detected on an actual flight); for instance, after take-off the landing-gears are retracted into their wheel wells in the fuselage, which makes a characteristic sound during the process. It is perhaps helpful to remember that the main gears involved, which themselves can weigh up to five tons, require a force of around 100 tons of hydraulic power to lift them, and that the undercarriage wheels can be rotating in excess of 150mph as they are retracted into their housing. This naturally makes some noise.

Pressurisation and ventilation All commercial jet aircraft are pressurised. With increasing altitude (and thinner air) planes go faster and further on each gallon of fuel, and air is gradually pumped into the cabin to warm it for passenger comfort and to keep the pressure and humidity as close as possible to take-off levels. You will hear a constant low-volume gushing sound as the air is changed in the cabin (every few minutes); variations in noise levels can occur, especially when individual blowers are switched on and off. As the system is powered indirectly by the engines, there may well be slight fluctuations in the constancy of the stream as the power source is varied.

Miscellaneous sounds

Depending on where you are sitting in the plane and upon which aircraft you are travelling, you may during the flight hear a lift mechanism in operation (for example, in the Lockheed L-1011 TriStar). Other in-flight noises that are never explained are the 'bongs' and 'dings' that are used to bring the passengers' attention to the fact that seat belt and no-smoking signs are in operation, but also indicate that the crew internal telephone system is in use. When you hear a bong or ding and no sign is illuminated, look around to see if the steward-stewardess is talking on the telephone. These signals, in addition, inform the crew to strap themselves in for

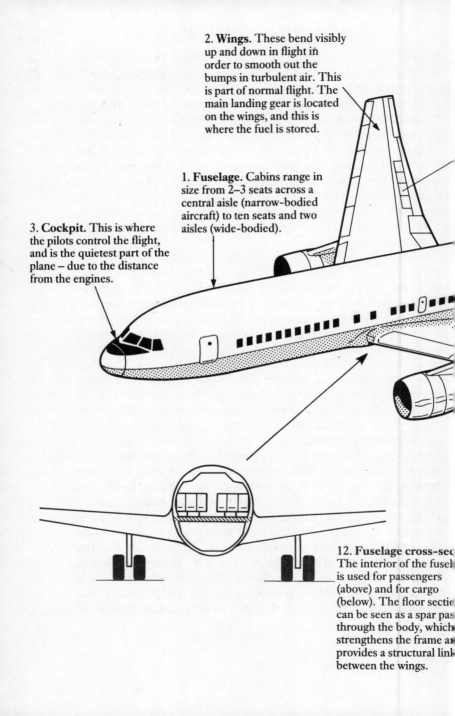

2. Wings. These bend visibly up and down in flight in order to smooth out the bumps in turbulent air. This is part of normal flight. The main landing gear is located on the wings, and this is where the fuel is stored.

1. Fuselage. Cabins range in size from 2–3 seats across a central aisle (narrow-bodied aircraft) to ten seats and two aisles (wide-bodied).

3. Cockpit. This is where the pilots control the flight, and is the quietest part of the plane – due to the distance from the engines.

12. Fuselage cross-sec The interior of the fusel is used for passengers (above) and for cargo (below). The floor sectic can be seen as a spar pas through the body, which strengthens the frame a provides a structural link between the wings.

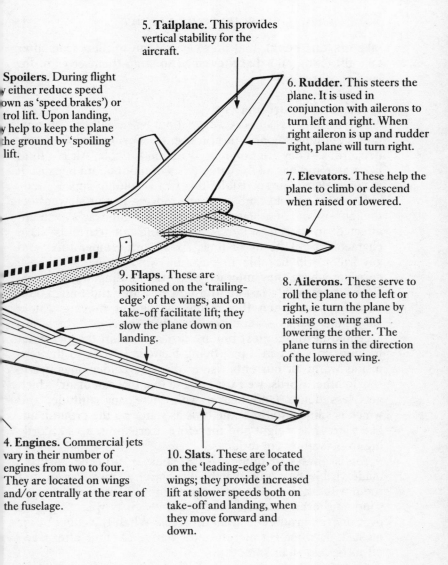

5. Tailplane. This provides vertical stability for the aircraft.

Spoilers. During flight ⊢ either reduce speed ⊢own as 'speed brakes') or ⊢trol lift. Upon landing, ⊢y help to keep the plane ⊢he ground by 'spoiling' ⊢lift.

6. Rudder. This steers the plane. It is used in conjunction with ailerons to turn left and right. When right aileron is up and rudder right, plane will turn right.

7. Elevators. These help the plane to climb or descend when raised or lowered.

9. Flaps. These are positioned on the 'trailing-edge' of the wings, and on take-off facilitate lift; they slow the plane down on landing.

8. Ailerons. These serve to roll the plane to the left or right, ie turn the plane by raising one wing and lowering the other. The plane turns in the direction of the lowered wing.

4. Engines. Commercial jets vary in their number of engines from two to four. They are located on wings and/or centrally at the rear of the fuselage.

10. Slats. These are located on the 'leading-edge' of the wings; they provide increased lift at slower speeds both on take-off and landing, when they move forward and down.

The control surfaces of an aircraft. Modern jets have a variety of adjustable surfaces, to control all aspects of their movement.

take-off (one bong), that they can get out of their seats after take-off (two), and that they need to strap themselves in for landing (three).

Weather and turbulence

Many anxious passengers worry about bad weather – storms, rain, lightning, fog and turbulence – believing that these are dangerous. They are not, merely uncomfortable. Air is a fluid like water and has all the same types of motion, but because it is not as dense, or so visible, this fact is seldom appreciated.

Currents of cold and warm air, moving fast or slow, affect the movements of a plane in exactly the same way as fish are affected in ocean waters. Water and air currents have characteristic patterns of flow, speed and temperature, and any sailor will be able to describe what happens to these currents where they interact with surrounding water. Consider a river with a fast central flow of water and think about what happens when this meets the slower moving waters along the banks – counter currents develop, which are accepted in this context but are just as valid in the air. What happens to water in a pan being heated? It rises to the top, just as warm air currents rise to displace colder ones in the sky. In other words, we exist on land in an 'ocean of air' which gets less dense (and heavy) with increasing altitude, and which is subject to the same laws as water on the ground: air, like water, has weight and therefore exerts pressures according to prevailing conditions.

Air is always in motion – just look at airborne particles made visible by a ray of light or cigarette smoke, even in a room without draughts. Air moving in rapid motion becomes wind, and even a steady wind becomes gusty when it passes over uneven ground or built-up areas. When travelling by air on such days, expect therefore the period of climb after take-off to be less than smooth.

Turbulence – bumpiness on a flight due to interference of air flow – can be compared to sailing on a choppy sea or driving over cobblestones, and can occur either in cloud or in clear air without any evidence of cloud. 'Air pockets' or empty spaces into which planes can fall do not exist. Turbulence in clouds, which are simply air containing so much moisture that they become visible, is the result of mixing unlike masses of air that lead to vertical currents, with warmer air rising above colder air. When colder air pushes in underneath warmer air, the turbulence level is increased, and it is particularly evident during a 'cold pressure front'.

The most extreme kind of turbulence in cloud is found within thunderstorms, which are composed of a series of localised 'cells', invariably produced by *cumulo-nimbus* clouds – the large black towering ones with an anvil-shaped head – and are accompanied by thunder and lightning. These can develop extremely fast and can grow so tall that they remain bathed in sunlight long after night has fallen on the earth's surface. Within storm clouds a column of rapidly expanding warm air creates an updraft of up to 100mph, whereupon ice particles – hailstones and granular snow pellets – are formed as the moisture condenses. During this process lightning occurs due to the accumulation of a strong negative charge in the bottom of the thundercloud, which also worries some passengers.

There is nothing to be afraid of, since an aircraft is a perfectly bonded metallic conductor. It is therefore impossible for a lightning strike to penetrate to the inside of the plane or interfere with the flying controls. All you would experience is an intense flash of light, a characteristic 'bang', and that's all. You are completely safe in a plane during lightning in the air or on the ground.

The second type of turbulence is called *clear air turbulence* (C.A.T.) and occurs when two air streams travelling at different speeds converge. At the interface the air becomes disturbed and choppy in the same way that on water a fast tide flowing against the wind will chop the surface into short waves. C.A.T. is not common, neither is it dangerous. Weather stations and weather radar on aircraft can detect rough air in clouds, but not C.A.T. All planes have radar which constantly scans the weather ahead for about 200 miles by bouncing signals off the water droplets contained in any storm clouds. This information is displayed visually and colour coded according to whether or not the droplets are present; if so, the central storm is depicted graphically in red – whereupon the pilot would make a request to air traffic control to fly around or above it. In other words, your pilot will never need to fly through a thunderstorm.

C.A.T. is not so predictable, but meteorological charts give pilots updated general information on areas around the world where it may be found – often above hot climates and mountainous regions. If it is encountered, pilots make a request to air traffic control to change altitude – getting out of such an environment is something a ship cannot do in a choppy sea! Because C.A.T. can occur with little if any forewarning, airlines advise passengers for safety and comfort (ie protection from banging your head on the luggage compartment, rather than anything more dramatic) to keep seat belts fastened loosely while seated. It is then easier to tighten them if conditions suddenly become bumpy.

In addition to changing altitude, another way of minimising the effects of turbulence is for the pilot to slow down the plane: aircraft manufacturers stipulate the speeds which they consider are optimum for such conditions, which are well practised by air crews on the training simulators on the ground prior to flying that type of plane.

Wind shear is another cause of turbulence, though rare. It is produced by irregular and gusty air which changes direction and force. It is also covered in pilot training, so can be dealt with effectively when it occurs.

Fog, along with mists and low cloud, can affect the feasibility of a visual landing approach. Such seasonal hazards, which in the past led to great inconvenience to passengers and airline schedules (missed appointments and connections, general delays, huge operational costs and disrupted flight operations), have virtually been eliminated due to the development of the automatic landing (or 'autoland') system. This involves a computerised automatic pilot on the aircraft which locks onto a radio beam sent out by the ground aerial of the instrument landing system, described previously. The autopilot flies the plane along this beam to touchdown, while controlling engine speed and angle of approach, all of which is monitored by the flight crew who can take over at a moment's notice in the event of a malfunction (very rare indeed). The fine details of this control are extremely impressive. The plane is lowered onto the runway gently by flaring the nose wheel, the spoilers (or speed brakes) are introduced, and on some aircraft the wheel brakes applied as and when required – all automatically.

There are various weather conditions against which an aircraft's performance can be measured, ie when an automatic landing can be undertaken. These range from Category 1 – visibility not less than 600 metres ahead and 60 metres above the runway, at which a pilot has to decide whether to land or not – to Category 3 (sub-divisions a, b and c) for very bad weather conditions. Category 3a requires a decision height of five to six metres and a runway visual range up to 200 metres; 3b requires a decision height of three metres and runway visual distance of 75 metres; and 3c no visual decision height or runway visual range at all. You can see CAT 1, 2, and 3 markers from the cabin as you taxi towards a runway. A number of types of aircraft can land in Category 3b conditions, but very few airports have an instrument landing system to cope with Category 3c conditions; these are extremely rare anyway.

Flight services which are disrupted in fog, heavy, driving rain and other bad weather are affected principally because either the aircraft or the airport does not have automatic landing equipment of the necessary level of sophistication and refinement.

To sum up: bad weather and turbulence may be uncomfortable, but the worst can be avoided or negotiated safely. There is no reason to feel threatened, for nothing worse will happen.

Air traffic control

As we have seen, jet aircraft operate most economically when cruising at high altitude, and aircraft travelling between airports – especially on short sectors – spend a significant proportion of time climbing and descending. They do this as quickly as they can so as to maximise cruising time, but are careful not to burn up too much fuel in doing so. Large numbers of aircraft are involved – including military and light aircraft – and it is the air traffic control service which gives advice and instructions to pilots to keep them safely separated from each other. In the cruise phase of flight this is at least five miles horizontal separation from another aircraft travelling at the same height, and 1,000ft vertical separation. Air traffic control also assists aircraft to take off, climb, descend and land promptly and safely, with the emphasis on the latter.

At *all* times an aircraft is in flight it is under radar control, and this control is transferred from sector to sector along the entire route until the final transfer to the airport of destination. Radar displays in air traffic control centres show all planes within their particular area of responsibility, and this information is updated every few seconds; in addition to showing each plane as a 'blip' on a screen, it contains other valuable data, including flight identification (airline and flight number), route (destination airport) and height.

Air traffic control enables airlines to run schedules reliably and to ensure that each aircraft flies safely along its selected route, deliberately and carefully separated from, but integrated with, all other aircraft movements taking place at the same time. Air traffic control is a service which makes excellent use of modern technology; it is run by a professional team of individuals, many of whom have pilot licences themselves – which gives them an even greater appreciation of the information requested by flight crews.

Safety aspects of flying

Anxious flyers concede that flying is very safe – on average, one fatal crash occurs per million flights worldwide – but

102

worry that it is *their* plane that is going to crash. Hence the need for a complete chapter on defusing the worry factor (see Chapter 6). Claims of manipulation of safety statistics by airlines, arguments about lowered standards in aircrew and aircraft maintenance and resistance to safety innovations on cost grounds, as being responsible for accidents are all myths when one examines the evidence. In a review of world airline safety and security for 1986, *Flight International* magazine reported (24 January 1987) that 'More than a quarter of all those people who died in airliners during 1986 lost their lives as a result not of airline, aircraft, equipment, or aircrew failure, but through deliberate acts intended to destroy them', and the report comments that the risk of such 'deliberate' disasters brought about by terrorism, sabotage or military action against civil targets has become as constant a threat as that of human error or equipment failure. But it takes only the total loss of one wide-bodied jet and passengers to upset the figures.

The report concludes that 'Airlines and airports are being chosen for their perceived skill and successfulness in security just as much as for those qualities in their flying operations, if not more.' However, though the number of accidents is still incredibly small, such pressure – which has considerable commercial implications too – might well keep it that way.

Of the accidents involving fatalities, excluding terrorism, statistics indicate that about three-quarters result from mistakes by aircrew – the majority at the time of take-off and landing. Next most common are failure in the airframe, engines and control systems, but those where air traffic controllers were held responsible are far less common.

Plane accidents are very, very rare: statistically, you would have to fly every day for about ninety-five years to have a chance of experiencing one as a passenger in a civilian aircraft. In any event, the majority of accidents are 'survivable' (that is, some or all of the passengers may survive the impact of a crash or a collision): in six out of ten accidents in which some people die, there are also some survivors. Statistics show that fire and smoke can be as great a hazard as the impact itself, and so familiarity with safety procedures on board is extremely sensible for peace of mind.

Firstly, read the safety instruction card carefully and pay close attention to the cabin crew demonstration of safety equipment and routines. I often notice passengers, many of whom are seasoned travellers and have seen it all before, ignoring these. But the specifics of equipment do alter and emergency exits are positioned differently in different kinds of aircraft, and can vary in type. Sometimes people disregard these routines and associated printed information as a way of denying that anything untoward could possibly happen to them, or as a way of validating for them the superstition and false belief that not paying attention ensures that there won't be an accident.

You can also do several other things to make flying safe for yourself and your fellow passengers: store your hand luggage away from aisles and exits; fasten your seat belt tightly if there are warnings about turbulence; do not smoke in the toilets; be ready to leave hand luggage behind and move quickly out of the plane if instructed to do so by the cabin staff. For those who are interested in finding out more about what actions you can take to increase your chances of surviving an accident, you are recommended to read Daniel A. Johnson's book, *Just in Case: A passenger's guide to airplane safety and survival* (published by Plenum Press, New York, 1984).

Lastly, your choice of seat should be determined strictly on the basis of whether or not you wish to smoke, whether you wish to have one close to a window or aisle, and how much leg room you require. Not in terms of 'Which is safer?'

Now the theory of flight – along with some related facts – has been discussed, it is appropriate to consider how to achieve physical relaxation before turning to combating distorted thinking (Chapter 6).

5

Learning to Relax

*If a man insisted always on being serious, and
never allowed himself a bit of fun and relaxation,
he would go mad or become unstable without knowing it.*
HERODOTUS

Now that you have identified your flying-related anxiety symptoms and learned about how an aircraft flies, it is necessary to select the techniques to help you physically relax. There is a wide variety of procedures available, but the following are likely to provide the means by which you can learn to relax most effectively.

The table overleaf lists techniques across the page and symptoms down the side. The most appropriate techniques for each kind of symptom are indicated by a large symbol, while other relevant procedures for the same symptom are shown by a smaller one.

It can be seen from the table that there is more than one technique for each symptom; those highlighted by a large symbol are recommended for practice first. Before starting the exercises, it is important to appreciate that physical symptoms may have a specific organic cause; for this reason it is advisable to consult your doctor before making the assumption that your physical symptoms are triggered by anxiety alone. An example of this is *otitis barotrauma* – a painful ear condition involving inflammation, which is adversely affected by pressure changes associated with ascent and descent during flying. The discomfort that this produces is directly

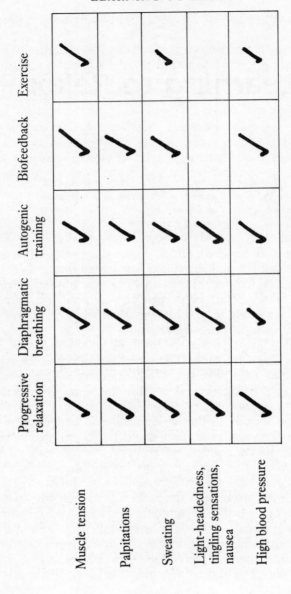

	Progressive relaxation	Diaphragmatic breathing	Autogenic training	Biofeedback	Exercise
Muscle tension	✓	✓	✓	✓	✓
Palpitations	✓	✓	✓	✓	
Sweating	✓	✓	✓	✓	✓
Light-headedness, tingling sensations, nausea	✓	✓	✓		
High blood pressure	✓	✓	✓	✓	✓

TABLE: Suitability of Different Relaxation Techniques According to Symptoms related to a physical problem, and in this case flying is contra-indicated.

Relaxation techniques basically deal with relaxing the body as opposed to *cognitive* techniques – the subject of Chapter 6 – which focus on how to use a variety of self-talk approaches to defuse anxiety where appropriate. It is likely that you will benefit most by using at least one technique from each category – a combination, say, of progressive relaxation and diaphragmatic breathing, if your symptoms comprise muscle tension and over-breathing, and rehearsing positive self-statements if your worries involve catastrophising and nega-tive monologues about air travel.

Before exploring the technique of relaxation further, it is recommended that you spend a preliminary period becoming aware of your bodily reactions across a variety of situations.

Body awareness

Body awareness is a necessary first step in the alleviation of anxiety. Most of us are more aware of our financial position, our next meal or the weather, than we are of the tension in our bodies.

Edmund Jacobson, an American psychologist earlier this century, found that a relaxed subject, even *thinking* about moving a limb, produced recordable muscle flexion in that limb. These were measurable only when the person was in a fully relaxed state, since they are obscured by general muscle tension. Moreover, he found that *all* thought is accompanied by low levels of activity in skeletal muscles – ie the muscular system over which a person has direct control. This is why they are sometimes referred to as 'voluntary' muscles; such activity is particularly noticeable around the eyes.

This and subsequent research demonstrated once and for all that if one wishes to relax the mind and the body it is crucial to relax *all* of the interacting systems of the body. This is achieved directly by relaxing the skeletal musculature, whereupon the central nervous system (ie brain and spinal cord) relaxes along with the various components of the

107

autonomic nervous system – the part that controls the functions of the *smooth* muscles and glands. Compared to skeletal muscle, smooth muscle is involuntary; it forms the walls of blood vessels and internal organs of the body, and is not under a person's control.

Several psychotherapists, including the founders of Gestalt Therapy (Fritz Perls) and Bio-energetics (Alexander Lowen), emphasise in their work that the body registers stress long before this comes to the level of consciousness. In other words, physical symptoms, notably muscular tension, are the body's way of signalling that you are under stress.

You need to be both internally and externally aware so that you can separate your environment from your physical reaction to it. Internal awareness comprises any physical sensation, either positive or negative, and consequent feelings. Much of this is not felt, since one's attention is usually directed externally, to the outside world, which includes stimuli to the five senses.

The following exercise will help to pinpoint areas of tension and facilitate body awareness:

1. Sit comfortably in a place where you are unlikely to be disturbed.
2. Focus on what you can see around you, and listen to sounds, and try to identify them (eg wind rustling in the trees, dog barking, lamp glowing in the room).
3. Turn to your body and attend to the state of your muscles, quality of breathing, any feelings of comfort/ discomfort (eg tenseness in shoulders, full stomach).
4. Alternate between focusing on internal v external awareness.

At odd times of the day try switching attention, as in 4, to make a distinction between internal state and external world. Then for the next two weeks keep a stress diary, using one column to describe your symptoms, one to note the time of day, another to specify what you were doing prior to and during the onset, and a last one to record what you said to yourself at the time. Include a rating from 0–10, where 0 = completely calm and relaxed and 10 = opposite extreme (ie very tense, panicky), as a way of quantifying the experience. This tension barometer can be used as a shorthand measure, whereby you can compare your state of relaxation before and after the following exercises.

PROGRESSIVE RELAXATION

Description and rationale

For over fifty years this technique, first described by Edmund Jacobson, has been the most popular non-pharmacological approach for promoting bodily relaxation and combating anxiety. The basic principle of progressive relaxation is that every tension serves a purpose and means something special to each person. Tensions are interpreted in a wide variety of ways depending on the person's perception and the significance of the meaning for the individual. The process involves the muscular contractions present during images and sensations, whereas the meaning of the event refers to the content of a person's thoughts. When flying is perceived as a threat, as it is for many anxious air travellers, muscle tension is a common reaction to any thoughts about taking a flight.

In technical terms, the tension sensation is described as the 'control signal', for it is a control of the neuromuscular circuits that execute the body's activities. More specifically, when a muscle tenses or contracts, the nerve receptors which are embedded in it become activated. This generates a series of nerve impulses which are carried to the brain. It is the muscle-nerve connection that embodies the control signal – the local indication of tension.

The ultimate goal of progressive relaxation is for the body to monitor rapidly all of these control signals, and to eliminate inappropriate tensions. Deep progressive relaxation of your muscles can reduce pulse rate and blood pressure, as well as decreasing perspiration and respiration rates. It requires no imagination, nor is it based on suggestion. By reducing physiological tension through deep muscle relaxation, it is incompatible with anxiety and is highly recommended for virtually every anxious flier.

Indications
There are two applications of tension control – prevention and therapeutic. It is possible to prevent the build up of tension by learning how to relax in active situations, but for those who already experience the distress of bodily tension, progressive relaxation can often reduce and eliminate the discomfort. Relaxing the skeletal muscles systematically by gradual lengthening of the muscle fibres extends to a state of relative calmness throughout the central nervous system. As a result, the viscera can relax – indicated by a lowering of blood pressure, reduction in pulse rate, and increased function of the gastro-intestinal tract. In other words, relaxing muscles effectively can also produce positive changes in related systems of the body. There is evidence that worrying thoughts can be eliminated by relaxing the speech muscles (tongue, jaw, lips, throat and cheeks) used in mental activity, and the eye muscles (to eliminate the visual components of thoughts), but this is likely to be achieved more reliably in combination with the self-talk strategies described in Chapter 6.

Limitations and contra-indications
Progressive relaxation training cannot be used to treat a physical condition or cure a viral infection, but it can be effective as an adjunct procedure to ease a patient's discomfort for any illness. Increasing a person's relaxation may well lessen the experience of distressing symptoms. However, there are a few physical problems that may be affected adversely by tensing various muscle groups, including arthritis, fibrositis and atherosclerosis. But apart from these conditions, relaxation is appropriate wherever *rest* is desirable.

Instructions

First of all, choose a quiet place in which to sit, or preferably lie, where you will not be interrupted (take the telephone off the hook, place a 'Do Not Disturb' sign on the door). Make sure the room is not too hot or cold, loosen any tight clothing and settle into a comfortable position. If you are sitting, take off your shoes, place both feet on the floor, and rest your arms alongside the arms of the chair. If you are lying down, preferably on your bed or the floor, do so on your back and rest your arms by your sides.

1. Close your eyes and take notice of your body and rhythm of breathing, and locate specific areas of muscle tension.
2. Switch your attention back to your breathing and make sure that you are breathing slowly – by pausing briefly between the in-breath and out-breath.
3. Breathe through your nose (*not* your mouth).
4. Breathe deeply, *not* shallowly, expanding your abdomen as you breathe in, and follow this immediately by raising your chest in order to fill your lungs with air. Hold your breath for a couple of seconds and then breathe out slowly, making sure both the muscles of your chest and abdomen are relaxed. If your habitual pattern of breathing is to use your mouth and/or chest in preference to your nose and abdomen, go directly to the next section on *Breathing* for further advice; and then return to this exercise.

If you find your mind wandering during these tasks, simply re-focus on your breathing and ensure you follow the above sequence. Then continue as follows.
5. Clench your right fist, tighten and tighten; concentrate on the tension in your fist, hand and forearm; hold the tension, and let go on an out-breath while saying under your breath the word *relax*. Feel the looseness in your right hand and compare this with how it felt when you were making a fist. Repeat this exercise with your

111

right hand and note again the contrast in sensation between tension and relaxation.

6. Repeat the procedure in 5 with your left hand, and then with both hands.

7. Next, bend your elbows and tense the muscles of your arms. Hold the tension, then relax by straightening your arms while at the same time reciting the word *relax*. Don't forget to relax on the out-breath.

8. In turn, tense and relax as above, also repeating each procedure, for each of the following parts of your body:

Back Arch your back upwards (or forwards if you are sitting).

Shoulders Press your head back.

Jaws Clench your teeth.

Tongue Press it against the roof of your mouth.

Forehead Wrinkle it by raising your eyebrows.

Stomach Imagine you are defending yourself against a punch.

Buttocks Pull them together.

Thighs Straighten your knee and make your legs stiff.

Calves Press your heels down and point your feet up.

Feet, ankles and toes Curl up your toes and press your feet down.

9. Now give your entire body an opportunity to relax, by tensing up all your muscles together and then letting go.

Timing

It is recommended that you practise progressive relaxation every day for 15–20 minutes, avoiding times immediately prior to bedtime or after a meal, and repeat this if time permits. Continue for about a week or until full relaxation is achieved.

'Letting go' exercise

Once you have mastered the tense-relax exercise and pin-pointed the muscle groups relevant to you, you can progress to an abbreviated version which involves monitoring the various muscle groups in your body and then letting go of any tension present, without tensing up before doing so. The value of the latter procedure is to highlight the contrast between tension and relaxation, which you will have learned by this stage. After checking out the state of your muscles, focus in turn on the muscle groups which are not fully relaxed and simply 'let go' of the tension during breathing out.

I suggest that you start by practising this exercise in relatively quiet and controlled situations – eg in your home when no one else is around – before applying it during other activities, and that you combine muscle groups as follows: a) both arms and both hands; b) neck and face; c) abdomen, back, chest and shoulders; and d) both legs and both feet. Relaxation using this sequence should take about ten minutes, and the optimum frequency is two or three times a day. Once you have pinpointed the specific muscles which generally become tense, you need only relax these rather than the others. This will cut down the time required to achieve a desirable level of relaxation.

This exercise can be repeated several times throughout the day, whenever you notice any muscle tension. It is very discreet and no one else need notice what you are doing.

Differential relaxation
This is the application of the 'letting go' exercises to a variety of situations which are associated with tension. Initially, they might be general day to day events, such as waiting in traffic, trying to contact a busy telephone number or working towards a tight deadline, but after a few days you need to apply the procedures to specific flight-related activities like, for example, booking your ticket, looking at pictures of aircraft or imagining that you are on a plane taxying towards the runway. During imagery sessions try and take in all the sensations – what the scene looks like, the people, colours, smells, movements and noises. (See the section on systematic desensitisation in Chapter 6 for further instructions about the use of imagery during relaxation.) It is most useful if you work

through less to more anxiety-provoking situations and imagery, in systematic fashion, and that you do not move from one scenario to the next until you have achieved bodily relaxation in the previous one. Furthermore, it is important for maximum benefit that you combine the right kind of breathing (stomach- rather than chest-centred) with these exercises. This is explained fully later in the chapter.

Potential problems and suggested solutions

Several problems which can interfere with relaxation training have been described in various psychological and medical books and journals, along with recommended solutions. The most common ones, which will help you to get the most out of deep muscle relaxation exercises, are described below. Your physical comfort is the initial concern so if you do find it difficult to relax while fully reclined – as one client did following a long-standing problem with his back – do not feel obliged to follow standard procedure, which involves lying in a supine position. By the same token, you may find (as another client did) that a different kind of tensing strategy to that of tightening your muscles – in his case lifting his leg slightly off the ground – works much better.

a) Intrusive thoughts This is probably the most disruptive factor during a relaxation session, when various intrusive (ie unwanted, repeated and perhaps resisted) thoughts lead to arousal and/or anxiety, and they are usually in evidence at the first session. They generate discomfort, fear or conflicts and can relate to flying or other concerns, such as relationship difficulties or financial problems. When the thoughts are about flying, it is necessary to follow the self-talk programme in Chapter 6, which involves learning how to talk to yourself more rationally about air travel. As for other stress-related thoughts, it is important to apply the Thought Stopping procedure, as well as adopt a Problem Solving approach, outside the relaxation sessions to defuse the problems (again see Chapter 6 for a full explanation of techniques).

Very occasionally, clients (usually male) worry when they

do a relaxation session in a group that they may become sexually aroused. Needless to say, the response should be allowed to subside as it eventually will.

b) Difficulty in relaxing specific muscle groups If you are having difficulty in relaxing specific muscle groups despite repeated attempts at using the standard procedure outlined above, the following alternative tensing strategies are available, according to the muscle group in question:

1. *Biceps (upper arms)* Try pressing your elbow down and inward towards your body. This leaves the lower arm and hand in a relaxed state.

2. *Forehead* Try frowning in an exaggerated fashion.

3. *Neck* Try pressing your head back against your chair, floor or bed.

4. *Chest, shoulders and upper back* Try pulling your shoulders upwards – equivalent to an exaggerated shrug.

5. *Abdomen* Try pulling your stomach in as far as possible, or push it outwards.

6. *Thigh* Try lifting your leg off the ground very slightly.

7. *Calves* Try pointing your toes away from your head.

If a particular muscle group where you experience tension has not been dealt with, you will need to develop a tensing strategy for that area and repeat the sequence as for other groups.

c) Unusual sensations during relaxation These involve feelings of disorientation in space, floating, loss of contact with positions of arms and legs, and are often accompanied by sensations of warmth, tingling, coolness in the limbs. They are usually experienced by those who are focusing on relaxation for the first time and those who have not achieved deep relaxation previously. Sometimes people feel frightened because they do not understand that these symptoms are commonly felt when learning to relax. Indeed, they demon-

115

strate that you are acquiring the ability to relax effectively. It is important to learn how to accept rather than fear such sensations, for nothing worse is going to happen.

If you still feel uncomfortable keep your eyes open during the exercises, look around the room and over your body, and then close your eyes again. Do this whenever these feelings occur and the discomfort will diminish with practice.

d) 'Losing control' during relaxation Feelings produced during relaxation need to be seen as pleasant experiences under *your* control. Reports of fear of tensing muscles, going 'mad' and 'losing control', usually relate to feelings of dissociation with one's body and a worry that something terrible will happen if you let go.

It is important to remind yourself that it is you who are in control of your own responses, and that although the sensations that relaxation produces may be new, they can be pleasant. Take your time to get used to the exercises; try on the first occasion simply to lie or sit comfortably, looking around the room and switching your attention from what you can see in it to your body and the state of muscle relaxation/ tension in different parts. You might even find it preferable to sit upright first of all. In the next session recline in your seat or lie flat on your bed, keeping your eyes open but turning off the lights in the room. In the session after that, close your eyes.

e) 'Internal arousal' This is where you have no muscle tension following a relaxation session, but you feel an internal sensation of arousal. It may be because some muscles are not under voluntary control and are thus not affected by the relaxation procedure. With practice it is likely that you will achieve more 'internal' relaxation, but it may be that you need to learn how to control your sweating, pulse rate or other autonomic responses (see other techniques in this chapter).

f) Sleep Falling asleep during a relaxation training session is common, especially when it is carried out early in the morning or after a busy day's activities, shortly after a substantial meal or immediately prior to retiring for the night. To avoid this happening, choose the timing of your session at other periods of the day, when you are more alert. If you find that you still go to sleep, reduce the relaxation session to only a few minutes at a time and make sure that you sleep for long enough during the previous night.

g) *Muscle cramps* This painful condition, resulting from contraction of muscles from strain, occurs most frequently in the calves and feet and should be avoided. This can be achieved by generating less tension for a shorter period of time, preferably less than five seconds for the feet.

If you do get cramp, stay in the reclined position with eyes closed, allow the rest of the body to remain as relaxed as possible, while moving only the affected muscles. Then continue with the tension-relaxation procedure, using a brief, 3–5 second tension cycle with the muscle group where the cramp had occurred.

h) *Movement* Body movements like stretching, fidgety actions of the arms, hands or feet, or relieving a momentary itch, are acceptable so long as the intention is to get more comfortable; but frequent and extensive movement throughout a relaxation session over a number of sessions can be a major barrier to achieving a state of muscle relaxation.

One way of dealing with this is to make sure that muscle groups are not moved once they have been relaxed. Check that you are following the instructions correctly and remember that slight and occasional movement is desirable, rather than absolute stillness which in itself can be tension provoking.

i) *Laughter or talking* It is not uncommon, particularly on the first session, for some people to find the procedures amusing and start laughing, and this is sometimes accompanied by vocalisations. If the session is conducted in a group setting, as with the author's Air Travel Anxiety Seminars, laughter and talking often signify tension relief and can facilitate subsequent relaxation. If practice is carried out individually then the novelty of the situation, coupled with a feeling perhaps of embarrassment, explains laughter on the first occasion. This subsides quickly and attention to the instructions is all that is required to achieve a desirable level of muscle relaxation.

j) External noise Under ideal circumstances, relaxation training should take place in a soundproof room, but this environment is virtually never available. Make sure, therefore, that all unnecessary noise – local traffic, telephones, other people etc – is minimised, even to the point of putting a notice on your door requesting not to be disturbed. If you are unable, for any reason, to eliminate such interference, then it is important that you use any external distraction as a trigger to focus attention back onto your muscle exercises. In due course, however, it will be constructive to relax actively in noisy locations, for travelling by air, in particular, is where such conditions prevail.

k) Spasms and tics These occur often in those who are initially very tense and who have had little experience of muscle relaxation exercises. Such twitches, jerks and tics are muscle spasms which are associated with relaxation and are common when people are about to go to sleep. Do not be concerned about these; they merely indicate that relaxation is progressing nicely and there need be no attempt to prevent them. The reason that they seem to be prominent is that ordinarily your level of consciousness (prior to sleep) is a lot less than during a relaxation session, when you are attending specifically to the state of your muscles.

l) Coughing and sneezing These can usually be ignored; they will not interfere with your ability to relax so long as you do not attempt to inhibit such behaviour, which would lead to increased muscle tension.

If you have a cold, it may be a good idea to postpone your relaxation session until after the symptoms have subsided, simply because the discomfort can affect both your motivation and ability to relax. However, if you are a heavy or moderate smoker you may well find that attempting to breathe deeply and hold your breath during relaxation triggers the characteristic smoker's cough. The best way to deal with this is to take a breath while tensing, but not to

118

inhale as deeply. Another way is to breathe out (not too force-fully) while tensing the relevant muscles, followed by resumption of normal breathing as these muscles are relaxed. If these instructions do not suppress the cough, it is recommended that you do not continue with the breath-holding aspect of the breathing technique.

Following the instructions

Be sure to do the exercises regularly, correctly and in sequence, and that you are relaxing all the tension at once rather than gradually. Remember that feelings follow behaviour, and that having a daily schedule where you give both space and time for relaxation will help you achieve the desired reduction in bodily tension. You should leave each session feeling better than when you started. If not, you may need to devote some more time or break the programme into smaller components, whereby you do not go to the next level until you have achieved relaxation in the last.

BREATHING EXERCISES

Description

One of the principal symptoms of the anxious flyer is a thoracic pattern of breathing, involving chest, rapid and shallow breathing and frequent sighs. This, as explained in Chapter 2, can lead to feelings of faintness, light-headedness, dizziness, excessive fatigue, palpitations, chest pains, sweating, nausea, paraesthesia or tingling sensations, and disturbances of consciousness. Diaphragmatic (ie stomach-centred) breathing exercises, which involve the diaphragm – the band of muscle across your abdomen – slow the respiration rate and stomach (rather than chest) movement, and are one of the most rapid and effective ways to neutralise tension and anxiety when used in combination with the self-talk strategies detailed in Chapter 6.

Few of us retain the healthy habit of effortless, peaceful breathing – look at any sleeping infant and that is the pattern that you will observe. As people get older, they often adopt a thoracic-centred breathing habit, which can be viewed as an emergency procedure since it prepares the person for a 'fight or flight' (ie avoidance or escape) action. When flying is construed as a threat, dangerous or unwanted and not controllable, then this kind of breathing pattern is likely to occur. The problem is compounded when tight clothing is worn, and on an aircraft the anxious flyer makes the situation worse by gripping the arms of the seat and leaning forward; this produces tension in your upper arms, across the chest and upper back – the muscles against which you must breathe. This style of breathing makes it difficult to reduce the tension, and so learning the diaphragmatic breathing technique is extremely desirable.

Rationale

Among the general population, research suggests that 6–11 per cent of people habitually hyperventilate: people who, physiologically speaking, can be easily tipped into producing respiratory symptoms regardless of the source of additional arousal – eg anxiety, exercise or excitement. There are more women than men with this condition (the ratio varying from 7:1 to 2:1) and a peak incidence among women in the 15–30 age group and in middle-aged men, both times of potential stress independently of air travel.

In attempts to compensate for the onset of symptoms, the increased use of thoracic muscles produces fatigue and chest pain (this is why some people complain mistakenly of coronary concerns) which can take different forms: sharp, flashing, left-sided discomfort, left-sided aching associated with local tenderness and a diffuse sensation of pressure over the heart. Palpitations may also accompany hyperventilation as well as breathlessness – ie not being able to get enough air into the chest or a feeling of gasping or choking, and an unproductive cough.

Hyperventilation occurs in disorders in which anxiety is prominent and is one of the main physiological responses to

120

stress. Over-breathing produces a low level of carbon dioxide in the blood, which makes the blood increasingly alkaline. This induces a narrowing of the blood vessels in the brain, a reduction in circulation and oxygenation, and therefore impairment of cerebral function. Some people also complain of cold hands or feet and sweating.

Indications

Breathing exercises are important during air travel because the air becomes thinner outside of the aircraft as you climb away from the earth's surface. At altitude the cabin is pressurised to the equivalent of 5–6,000ft above sea level, which means that there is less oxygen than you are probably used to; but importantly, there is always plenty for everyone's needs. You would not ordinarily feel the difference unless you breathed rapidly and shallowly, which is what happens when you get anxious. Diaphragmatic breathing will enable you to move more air with less effort, and thereby compensate for the reduced pressure.

In addition to following the instructions below you are advised to:

1. *Drink non-carbonated drinks* Gases expand at altitude and carbon dioxide may reduce the availability of oxygen. However, if you do hyperventilate, then breathing over a carbonated drink is sensible.

2. *Avoid drinking alcohol* Alcohol lowers the oxygen in your bloodstream and makes it more difficult for you to replace it. It also has double the effect that it does on the ground – ie makes you tipsy at altitude much more quickly than the same amount would at sea level.

3. *Avoid smoking tobacco* Carbon monoxide produced from smoking reduces the oxygen-carrying capacity of the blood. If you must smoke, try to cut down, for peripheral blood vessels are constricted due to this and this lowers the oxygen rate even further.

4. *Sit back in your seat* Place a pillow (supplied by air-

121

lines on longer journeys) in the small of your back; this will stretch your diaphragm and facilitate stomach breathing. After take-off, and when the seat belt sign is switched off, recline the back of your seat and keep this position throughout the cruise phase of the flight, unless you are instructed otherwise. This will probably be due to temporary turbulence and need cause you no concern.

Limitations and contra-indications

There are no restrictions to using diaphragmatic breathing exercises; however, make sure not to hold your breath for any length of time, for this will lead to a build-up of carbon dioxide in the blood, which in turn can lead to a lowering of consciousness. Co-existing respiratory diseases, such as asthma or chronic obstruction airways disease, need to be excluded for which advice from a medical practitioner is essential. It is perfectly possible to fly with these conditions so long as appropriate treatment is being followed. Stomach breathing will complement this.

Instructions

1. Breathing awareness exercises
1. Loosen all tight clothing.
2. Lie on your back on your bed or floor – with your legs straight and slightly apart, and your arms by your sides. Close your eyes.
3. Attend to your breathing and focus on the differential movements of your chest and stomach by placing your left hand on the former and your right hand on the latter. Is your chest hand moving more than your stomach hand? Or vice versa? Or do you have a mixed pattern where both are moving equally? Is the movement minimal or more pronounced?
4. Are you breathing through your nose and/or mouth? Is this typical for you?
5. Can you hear your breath?

122

6. Are you breathing fast or slow?
7. Now place your left hand on your chest and your right hand on your stomach and repeat number 3.

This exercise will establish your pattern of breathing. If your chest hand is moving more than the stomach one or there is little movement or both are moving equally, or you can hear your breathing which is fast, or you are breathing via your mouth, then you need to practise the diaphragmatic breathing exercises which follow.

2. Re-breathing exercises – the 'paper bag' approach

This technique is recommended if you reach a high state of arousal and are hyperventilating. It is a simple, safe, effective and short-term measure, and involves re-breathing exhaled breath by placing a bag – a paper one is usually most handy for this – over your mouth. It serves to increase the amount of carbon dioxide in your body, which you need to reverse the symptoms of light-headedness etc. You will always find a paper bag in front of your airline seat, intended of course for travel sickness.

As a preliminary exercise on the ground, you can try deliberately over-breathing for up to three minutes, which will reproduce your symptoms. These can be brought under control right away by re-breathing into a paper bag, or breathing diaphragmatically in the manner described below.

3. Diaphragmatic breathing exercises

1. Lie down on your back on the floor or your bed. Place a small cushion behind the small of your back to extend your diaphragm abdomen.
2. Place your left hand on your chest and your right hand on your stomach. The aim of the exercise is for your stomach hand to rise during every breath in, and fall on every breath out. Your chest hand should remain still, otherwise you are breathing thoracically.
3. Choose a spot on the ceiling and concentrate on it,

though be aware of the movement of your hands.

4. Breathe through your nose only, and do so without making a noise. If you can hear your breathing, you are doing it too forcefully.

5. Breathe in deeply and slowly.

6. Pause between the in-breath and out-breath. Say the word *relax* under your breath during the pause.

Timing

Try and put aside 5–10 minutes twice a day for a week, to get used to this exercise. Then practise the technique in a sitting position for a few days and apply the routine whenever you notice your breathing has shifted to a thoracic mode.

Potential problems and suggested solutions

a) If you have problems in getting your diaphragm to move, place both arms over your head, or position your hands around the nape of your neck. These manoeuvres stretch the diaphragm muscle and help to induce stomach breathing.

b) Those suffering from sinus problems may find it preferable to adopt the following routine which uses an alternate nostril breathing exercise:

1. Sit or stand comfortably.

2. Place the index finger of your right hand on your forehead.

3. Press your right nostril with your right thumb.

4. Breathe in slowly and soundlessly through your left nostril.

5. Next, press your left nostril with your right ring finger, while at the same time letting go of your right nostril by removing your right thumb.

6. Breathe out slowly and silently and deeply through your right nostril.

7. Breathe in through your right nostril.

8. Press your right nostril with your right thumb, and let go of your left nostril.

124

9. Breathe out through your left nostril.
10. Breathe in through your left nostril.

Do this routine ten times. Use your left hand instead of your right if you are left-handed.

If you feel the presence of any tension in your body during the day, take a deep breath, make sure your muscles are relaxed and start to breathe diaphragmatically.

c) There is increasing evidence that caffeine can exacerbate physiological symptoms of anxiety, so cut down your intake of coffee and tea to no more than five cups per day.

You will find that learning to breathe diaphragmatically, to breathe slowly and deeply, will be a valuable device for defusing tension rapidly and effectively.

AUTOGENIC TRAINING

Description and rationale

Autogenic (ie self-regulation or self-generation) training is a systematic set of exercises developed in Berlin earlier this century by two physicians, Johannes Schultz and Wolfgang Luthe. It grew out of research into hypnosis where subjects were able to put themselves into a trance that had the effect of reducing tension, tiredness and headaches, and made their limbs feel warm and heavy. Autogenic training is effective in combatting stress through active control of the autonomic nervous system by learning verbal cues to relax, but in contrast to progressive and deep muscle relaxation it involves no direct instructions to tense and relax your muscles. Your body is trained to respond to specific sub-vocal statements suggesting warmth and heaviness in your limbs, as a means of reducing physical arousal and tension. In other words, relaxation develops out of a 'passive concentration' on visual, auditory and body images, that produces desirable physiological changes such as low pulse rate and heaviness in your limbs.

125

Indications

Autogenic training has been found to be effective in the treatment of a variety of physical disorders, including those affecting the circulatory system (eg rapid or irregular heart beat, high blood pressure, headaches, and cold extremities), gastro-intestinal tract (eg constipation, diarrhoea, and ulcers) and the endocrine system (eg thyroid problems), but it is also of considerable benefit in the alleviation of general anxiety, irritability and fatigue, common symptoms of the fearful flyer. It can increase your ability to deal with stress and help to normalise sleeping irregularities.

Limitations and contra-indications

Before starting Autogenic Training it is advisable to have a physical examination from your physician and discuss what physiological effects the exercises are likely to have on you. Those with heart disease, diabetes and related conditions need to be medically supervised since changes in blood pressure are sometimes reported, and these require close monitoring.

The procedure is not very suitable for young children or for those with severe mental or emotional problems, and is counter-productive in the person who lacks motivation. Daily effort is necessary to learn psycho-physiological control, and to maintain it requires regular commitment of time. Those taking medication for stress-related disorders (eg for hypertension or thyroid imbalance) need to attend to dosage levels, since Autogenic Training generally leads to physiological improvements through the acquisition of self-regulatory skills and therefore a reduction in the level of medication might need to be discussed with your physician.

Increased physiological relaxation as a result of Autogenic Training may bring to consciousness emotionally filled sensations, and if this happens it is recommended that you engage in a series of brief sessions (lasting five minutes or so only) during the day rather than one or two longer sessions. If you find that these experiences persist, either consult your

126

physician or seek the advice of a professional Autogenic Training instructor from your local directory.

Instructions

Select a warm, quiet and private place where you will not be distracted or interrupted. Choose *one* of the following three positions as your preferred posture for learning the training exercises on the basis of which feels most comfortable:

1. Sit back in a high-backed armchair with your arms along the arms of the chair, and make sure your legs are uncrossed, **or**
2. Sit on a chair with your head stooped forward, feet slightly apart, arms resting on your thighs, and hands slightly clasped between your legs, **or**
3. Lie flat on your back on bed or floor with head supported. Point your toes outward, rest your arms by your sides, and place your hands – palms down – on the surrounding surface.

Scan your body to check that the position you have chosen is free of tension. If not, make sure that your limbs are supported and that they are not over-stretched.

Take your time, and simply focus on doing the exercises properly. The essence of this approach is to adopt an attitude of 'passive concentration', whereby you focus on each exercise in turn without specific expectations about consequences. There are six themes, each of which will introduce a verbal formula, that you keep in mind while you concentrate on different parts of your body in sequence. The verbal expressions need to be repeated under your breath, over and over, and if you get distracted just acknowledge this and continue.

Passive concentration is a skill that requires learning and so do not be surprised if your mind wanders at first. It is typical for symptoms, described as 'autogenic discharges', to occur during this process; these are distracting but are normal occurrences. They can include involuntary movements, irritability, tingling, feeling emotional, and visual hallucinations. Simply follow the programme, for they will go away.

Repeating phrases is helpful because it keeps them in mind, but this needs to be complemented by imagery as the part of the brain that controls the physical processes of relaxation – the limbic system – does not understand language too well. It is necessary, therefore, to translate the content of the phrase into some kind of image. One such phrase is 'my arms and hands are heavy and warm', so by imagining what it would actually feel like if they did feel heavy or warm helps to bring about the desirable changes. You may find a particular visual image works for you – for example, imagine you are lying on a tropical beach, sinking into golden sand, with the sun's rays over your body, or holding your hands close to a log fire. Or perhaps that you are standing under a warm shower, lying on a heating pad, or even holding a warm cup of your favourite beverage. You can also imagine that your limbs are made of heavy lead, or that weights are attached to your arms and legs and these are gently pulling them down.

Find out which impression appeals to you as a relaxing image, and use it as your passport for autonomic quiescence. This will happen with continued practice.

The six standard verbal themes involve:

1. Heaviness (associated with muscle relaxation).
2. Warmth (associated with automatic relaxation).
3. Heart beat regulation.
4. Respiration.
5. Solar plexus (ie the complex of nerves situated at the pit of the stomach).
6. Forehead.

You can learn the first two themes separately, but often these can be combined effectively. The best way to do this is to record the following instructions on your personal cassette recorder, leaving sufficient time between the statements for you to repeat them to your self with the associated imagery. The modified Autogenic Training phrases which follow (by psychologist Alyce Green in the USA* and slightly changed by the author) include the 'mind-quieting' phrases she developed specifically for this purpose:

1. I feel quite quiet.
2. I am beginning to feel quite relaxed.
3. My feet feel heavy and relaxed.
4. My ankles, my knees, and my hips feel heavy, relaxed, and comfortable.
5. My solar plexus, and the whole central portion of my body, feel relaxed and quiet.
6. My hands, my arms, and my shoulders feel heavy, relaxed and comfortable.
7. My neck, my jaws, and my forehead feel relaxed. They feel comfortable and smooth.
8. My whole body feels quiet, heavy, comfortable and relaxed.
9. (Continue alone for a minute.)
10. I am quite relaxed.
11. My arms and hands are heavy and warm.
12. I feel quite quiet.
13. My whole body is relaxed and my hands are warm, relaxed and warm.
14. My hands are warm.
15. Warmth is flowing into my hands; they are warm, warm.
16. I can feel the warmth flowing down my arms and into my hands.
17. My hands are warm, relaxed and warm.
18. (Continue alone for a minute.)

Principles and Practice of Stress Management edited by Robert L. Woolfolk and Paul M. Lehrer, Guilford Press, New York, 1984

19. My whole body feels quiet, comfortable and relaxed.

20. My mind is quiet.

21. I withdraw my thoughts from the surroundings, and I feel serene and still.

22. My thoughts are turned inward, and I am at ease.

23. Deep within my mind I can visualise and experience myself as relaxed, comfortable and still.

24. I am alert, but in an easy, quiet, inward-turned way.

25. My mind is calm and quiet.

26. I feel an inward quietness.

27. (Continue alone for a minute.)

28. The relaxation and reverie is now concluded. My whole body is re-activated with a deep breath.

29. I feel life and energy flowing through my legs, hips, solar plexus, chest, arms and hands, neck and head. The energy makes me feel light and alive.

30. Stretch and get up slowly.

Follow daily practice of this routine until you learn to achieve some control over bodily, emotional and mental functions. It is necessary to incorporate breathing exercises (see previous section) to establish deep diaphragmatic breathing, to lower your breathing rate to 4–6 cycles per minute, and to learn to exhale, let go and breathe slowly and deeply as a way of de-stressing yourself. Remember that gasping and holding your breath is a way of blocking feelings; rapid, shallow breathing occurs during times of anxiety, and awareness of this indicates the necessity of inducing a diaphragmatic pattern of breathing.

When you have learned the above training phrases and found them effective, it is appropriate to add the following to your taped sequence:

1. My heartbeat is calm and regular.

2. My solar plexus is warm.

3. My forehead is cool.

130

Do not forget to leave sufficient space on your recording for you to repeat the phrases.

The above phrases are known as the 'standard' themes, but there are, in addition, special ones which Schultz called 'organ specific formulae' to deal with specific difficulties. For instance, if your face flushes when you get anxious, you can prepare indirect phrases such as 'my feet are warm' or 'my forehead is cool', which facilitate passive concentration on a part of your body to mobilise blood away from your face.

There are meditational components of Autogenic Training which focus on mental rather than physical functions, but I suggest that you read the relevant section of Chapter 6 for further guidance on meditation.

Timing

It is recommended that you spend several weeks learning the standard Autogenic Training exercises, twice a day, 10–20 minutes on each occasion. Once you are familiar with the routine you can incorporate the phrases into your day-to-day activities whenever you feel stressed, particularly prior to making and during any journey by air. If you only have a brief time available for practice, concentrate solely on the warmth and heaviness phrases and on your breathing and heart rate.

Potential problems and suggested solutions

If you are finding it difficult to attend to the autogenic phrases without distraction, develop some visual images to intensify the sensations. Use 'thought stopping' whenever your mind wanders or you have an intruding and unwanted thought. Simply say to yourself 'Stop' under your breath, and return to the autogenic phrases/images.

BIOFEEDBACK METHODS

Description and rationale

Biofeedback refers to the use of instrumentation to learn

131

voluntary control over your automatic nervous system – the system which regulates all the bodily functions traditionally thought to be uncontrollable: heart rate, blood pressure, muscle tension, brain wave activity, skin surface temperature and sweating response. Biofeedback equipment monitors selected channels of response which can be detected by electrodes and transformed into visual or sound signals. Any bodily change triggers an external signal, such as a needle reading or an auditory tone. When you are connected by a lead to the equipment, it is possible to see and/or hear the continuous monitoring of feedback of your selected bodily functions. This information is then used to see how effective various strategies you adopt are in changing the response in the desired direction.

The technique was developed in the USA in the 1960s, following pioneering animal research by Neal Miller, and it was not long before electronic biofeedback was applied in a clinical setting, where the object of such training was for the patient to achieve control over biological response systems that have been operating maladaptively and beyond conscious control.

There are three stages in biofeedback training:

1. *Awareness* that the response is maladaptive (ie not productive), and realisation that particular thoughts as well as bodily events can influence this;
2. *Control* of the response using the external signal as indication of progress; and
3. Learning to *transfer* the control developed into general life situations, as well as travelling by plane.

Biofeedback instruments provide results immediately. For example, in the measurement of sweating activity, electrodes are placed over the tips of the forefinger and thumb of either hand, which pick up tiny electrical signals that vary according to general arousal level (ambient temperature needs to be controlled so as not to interfere with this response). Breathing rapidly and shallowly, or thinking about taking a flight, may well lead to either a high-frequency tone or an extreme meter reading, depending on the mode of feedback (aural or visual). When relaxation takes place, the tone or needle is likely to go down – ie the signal lets you know without delay whether you are moving in the right direction. This signal is your guide to the effectiveness of your chosen relaxation technique.

You will discover by trial and error whether progressive muscle relaxation exercises, diaphragmatic breathing exercises, cognitive techniques (Chapter 6) or exercise facilitate the relaxation process. Biofeedback equipment will provide an instant measure of your progress.

The principal channels of autonomic response available for biofeedback training are:

a) Electromyographic (ie muscle) or EMG.
b) Temperature.
c) Galvanic skin (ie sweating) or GSR.
d) Brain wave activity or EEG.
e) Pulse rate.

Inexpensive monitoring equipment can be purchased for home use (one way of finding out about this is to check the advertisements in psychological journals and magazines), but they only measure one channel of response, usually sweating or skin conductivity. These devices provide a rough estimate of certain bodily functions, which generally include sweating, temperature, muscle and pulse rate. Simply choose the channel of response which is relevant for you – if you sweat when tense, you need a GSR device; if you experience muscle tension, then an EMG is right for you, and so on. Clinical psychologists often use more sensitive and accurate equipment, and you may find it preferable to consult a specialist for this kind of training rather than pursue this approach by yourself.

a) Electromyographic (EMG) training measures skeletal muscle tension, and usually the following muscles are chosen because they respond whenever you are stressed:

1. *Frontalis* – the forehead muscle responsible for frowning, which contracts when you are stressed;
2. *Trapezius* – leads to shoulder tightening and tense shoulders when anxious; and
3. *Masseter* – controls jaw tightening, when tense, angry or stressed.

b) *Temperature training* involves measuring surface skin temperature variations on fingers, hands or feet, using a small electrode which comprises a heat sensitive semi-conductor. When you are anxious, skin temperature declines due to constriction of the peripheral blood vessels and leads to a reduced blood flow to the extremities, ie cold hands and feet. When you are stressed, blood is diverted to the heart for fight or escape from the situation. Therefore, increasing skin temperature will have the opposite effect and is likely to induce feelings of relaxation.

c) *Galvanic skin response (GSR) training* Sweating response is a widely used measure of emotional arousal and is the basic physiological information obtained from 'lie detectors'. When you become anxious your sweat glands become more active; the equipment records (in millivolts) the electrical potential of your skin, produced by the natural metabolism of cells, which increases with anxiety. GSR training helps you to gain control of your autonomic nervous system by monitoring the activity of your sweat glands.

d) *Electro-encephalographic (EEG) training* There is a particular brain wave state called 'alpha' which is associated with calmness and relaxation. EEG biofeedback training helps you to become aware of the feelings related to alpha waves – around ten cycles per second – with a view to learning how to recreate the conditions that accompany this state.

e) *Pulse rate training* Here beats per minute are measured, which change according to your state of anxiety or relaxation.

Blood pressure can also be monitored, but usually this cannot be done using equipment designed for home use. Relatively speaking, the lower the heart rate or blood pressure the higher the degree of relaxation.

Indications
Biofeedback helps to pinpoint autonomic problems and provides an objective assessment of the effectiveness of intervention strategies used to modify unwanted responses. The fact that you learn how to control these responses emphasises the importance of taking charge of your own bodily functions in the alleviation of anxiety about air travel, rather than feeling unable to influence these unwanted symptoms in any way.

Limitations and contra-indications
Biofeedback training requires instrumentation that may not be readily available. In any event, it is far more useful as a way of finding out which relaxation techniques work for you rather than an alternative to the others described in this chapter. Once you have mastered the method relevant to your requirements, you need not use the biofeedback equipment further. However, some people prefer to take their device on an air journey to help them concentrate on active relaxation prior to and during the flight itself.

Caution must be exercised with diabetic individuals, for rapid relaxation using biofeedback could result in a much decreased need for insulin. In this situation, training needs to be conducted under medical supervision.

Instructions
After having selected and obtained your biofeedback device it is advisable, first of all, to set the tone or visual signal to a low level. Breathe shallowly and rapidly several times and see what happens to your response. In all probability the level will have increased suddenly and dramatically, indicating the arousing effects of thoracic breathing. Once the level has

returned to base-line, think about taking a flight and rate your response. Chances are that this has been substantial, which highlights the importance of dealing with your negative thoughts about flying (see Chapter 6 for details of cognitive procedures).

Next, set the signal level to the high end of the scale and select one or two relaxation techniques, depending upon your particular bodily reactions to flying, and find out what works in bringing it down. When you can do this reliably, practise the technique without using the biofeedback equipment.

Timing

Practise for 20–30 minutes on a daily basis until you find what combination of techniques is effective for you in bringing selected autonomic response levels down. These are your personal set of procedures that need to be rehearsed regularly, as well as in situations in imagination and in practice that are anxiety-provoking both prior to and during journeys by air.

Dealing with setbacks and problems

To reduce the likelihood of setbacks and problems in biofeedback training it is recommended that you contact a clinical psychologist experienced in this technique for a preliminary assessment session, where a personal programme can be formulated for you and instruction given on how to use the equipment properly and where to purchase it.

If, for any reason, biofeedback instrumentation is not available, you can always monitor your breathing and pulse rates prior to, and following, relaxation exercises, which will give you a relevant measure of change.

EXERCISE

Description and rationale

Regular exercise is an effective way of producing both bodily and mental relaxation. It provides a means of reducing muscle tension, general physiological arousal, and helps to empty the mind of stressful preoccupations. Concentration and sleep are improved, mood is elevated, and you have a reduced risk of developing coronary heart disease, especially when associated with healthy dietary patterns (ie low animal fats, salt free, and high fibre).

As you are aware, when you are stressed about flying, or other situations for that matter, predictable bodily changes take place: your heart beats faster, blood pressure rises, breathing quickens and becomes more shallow, muscles become tense, and adrenalin is secreted into the bloodstream along with fats and sugars to prepare you for dealing with the perceived threat. When we are physically fit, we can deal with such stresses and strains much more effectively: your responses to such stimuli are slower and less extreme, blood circulation is improved, blood pressure is lower, less fats are released into the bloodstream, and both lung capacity and muscular strength are enhanced. The heart works more efficiently with less effort, and has a superior pumping capability.

At a psychological level, certain types of prolonged exercise are said to be particularly effective due to the release of brain chemicals called *endorphins*, which act both as mediators of pleasurable states and serve to reduce the perception of painful sensations.

There are essentially two kinds of physical exercise: *aerobic* and *anaerobic*. The former refers to a variety of activities, such as running, swimming, cycling and dancing, that stimulate heart and lung activity for a period of time sufficiently long to produce beneficial changes in the body. They make you work hard and by doing so demand lots of oxygen – that's why they are called 'aerobic'. The goal is to increase the maximum amount of oxygen that your body can process within a given time, called your *aerobic capacity*, which is dependent upon your ability to:

1. Breathe rapidly large quantities of air;

2. Mobilise large volumes of blood; and
3. Deliver effectively oxygen to all parts of your body.

In other words, it depends upon efficient lungs and good respiratory muscles, a strong heart with good pumping efficiency, good general circulation, an increased amount of haemoglobin (making the blood a more efficient oxygen carrier), and muscles throughout the body with good tone. Aerobic capacity is the best single index of your overall physical fitness and needs to be determined by your local fitness assessment centre before embarking on any of the exercises described below.

Anaerobic exercises are low intensity activities that are neither sufficiently vigorous nor prolonged to produce such a training effect. They do not, therefore, benefit your cardio-vascular system, but are designed to increase your flexibility (mobility of your joints and strength of your muscles) and are complementary to aerobic exercises. If you are starting out to exercise for the first time or after an extended rest from such pursuits, these will help you to prepare for the ones which do influence your aerobic capacity. Such low intensity exercises include everyday activities like slow walking, lifting objects, shopping, and light gardening.

Indications
Exercise comes in a variety of forms where psychological and physical benefits can be enjoyed. If you are a non-exerciser, ask yourself the following questions to see if it will be suitable for you:

1. Are you more than a few pounds overweight?
2. If so, would you like to lose some weight permanently?
3. Do you smoke?
4. If so, would you like to stop smoking?
5. Do you feel you are not in the physical condition you used to be?
6. Would you like to get fit again?

138

7. Would you like to feel more relaxed?
8. Are you often rushing around, and don't have the time to unwind?

If you answered yes to most of these questions, exercise is right for you. However, if you find physical exercise worse than a visit to the dentist, perhaps you need to concentrate rather on the other relaxation techniques.

Limitations and contra-indications

Do not start an aerobics training programme if you are not used to such exercises, are overweight or have any medical condition, without consulting your physician first. If you are an extremely sedentary person begin with low intensity exercise such as walking, and be selective about what you eat and drink. If you smoke, try and cut down. Stop exercising if you experience chest pain, dizziness, breathlessness or palpitations, and see your doctor.

Instructions
Aerobic exercises

For health reasons, make sure you do not exceed the maximum recommended heart rate for your age, which is determined by subtracting your age in years from 220 – eg if you are 40, your maximum allowable heart rate is $220 - 40 = 180$ beats per minute. During aerobic exercises it is desirable to train at about 70–75 per cent of your age-related maximum rate, to obtain the best cardio-respiratory benefits.

Keep a daily diary to document your progress – eg time and distance if running – as well as pulse rate information. Do not step up the demands until you have achieved the appropriate level of pulse rate. There are four places where this can be taken: at your wrist, temple, side of your neck (between your Adam's apple and the large muscles at the side), and over your heart. Count the number of beats over a period of fifteen seconds, and multiply this by four for the rate of beats per minute.

Always warm up for five minutes prior to your chosen exercise, followed by a warm down for five minutes immediately after it. Try first of all brisk walking, jogging, running or swimming, making sure to wear the correct clothes and footwear for protection against injury. During the exercise, your large skeletal muscles tense and relax in sequence, which stimulates the blood flow through your cardio-vascular system. Monitor your pulse rate every five minutes during the exercise so that you are sure to keep within your physiological limits.

Anaerobic exercises
There are three types of low intensity exercises from which to choose, depending on what you want to achieve:

Isometric, which involves contraction of muscles against resistance – eg pushing your hands together at chest height while sitting down, or against a wall. This technique does not require movement and is therefore very suitable while travelling by plane. One airline (Finnair) has an audio channel in-flight with such a programme of exercises.
Isotonic involves contraction of muscles, and includes movement. Lifting light weights is the most common version of this type of exercise and can help to tone muscles and, if so desired, increase power and endurance.
Calisthenics help to increase your flexibility by stretching major muscle groups, and include sit-ups and touching your toes.

Timing
Do the anaerobic exercises every day, and the aerobic exercises every other day, preferably for twenty minutes at least. Try to programme them so that they happen automatically, like eating, for if you wait until you are in the mood, they may not occur at all.

140

Potential problems and suggested solutions

If you find it difficult to establish a regular routine for exercising, try attending a fitness training centre, where you can obtain your fitness profile and a personalised programme which will be run under supervision.

If you are worried about triggering a heart attack by exercise, then consult your physician who can arrange a stress test after a physical examination, which will indicate the status of your heart and the appropriate exercise programme for you. The key question is not *whether* exercise, but *what kind* of exercise is suitable for you.

Exercise is not just for the very young and athletic; it is for all ages and shapes, as you will see from visiting your local physical fitness centre.

Perhaps you feel that you cannot make enough time for exercise. 'Cannot' actually means 'will not', and simply conveys the impression that you have not given it a sufficiently high priority. If you want to go to the theatre, you make the time; exactly the same reasoning applies to exercise – providing you view the consequences of exercise to be worthwhile *and* perceive these goals to be attainable.

6
Dealing with the Worry Factor

Present fears
Are less than horrible imaginings.
WILLIAM SHAKESPEARE

From the previous two chapters you will have some appreciation of the theory and practicalities of flight, and know how to
relax physically. Anxiety about flying has been presented
either as a concern people have about what might happen to
themselves (eg panic or feel out of control) *or* to the aircraft
(eg turbulence or crashing). The crucial factor which under-
pins these concerns is determined by how you *perceive* flying,
and *not* the external reality of the situation. When flying is
considered to be threatening or dangerous, feeling worried is
entirely appropriate – in the same way that if you thought you
could catch AIDS by kissing someone, mouth to mouth
contact would make you extremely apprehensive, to say the
least. This chapter will teach you how to defuse distressing
thoughts about air travel and replace them with rational,
alternative ones, so that you can then let go and feel excited,
bored or neutral about it – just like the rest of us.

The first task is to become aware of your thought processes
and for some this is all that is necessary to start thinking
differently about flying. Such observations facilitate both a
distancing from negative thoughts and a measure of objectivity that otherwise might not be possible. Your anxiety is
probably restricted to periods leading up to and during a
flight, and so capturing your worries at these times is crucial;

when there is no flight on the horizon many anxious flyers view air travel with equanimity, so their thoughts at this time are not a good barometer of their true feelings about flying. But suggest a trip and that all changes.

Bringing frightening automatic thoughts into awareness makes it possible to modify them; passive acceptance of them simply keeps the problem alive, for it is *you* who is making yourself anxious not the aircraft. Many anxious flyers ask *why* they are fearful or cannot control their feelings about air travel, and have the false expectation that an answer will resolve their conflict. It will not; in any event the determinants of such problems are usually complex and multiple and generally lost in the mists of time; rather, a different set of factors – the ones that keep it alive – need to be scrutinised carefully. The question 'Why am I afraid?' needs to be replaced by 'What am I afraid of?' and 'Under what circumstances does this occur?'

Approach what makes you frightened and eventual confrontation enables you to pinpoint relevant trigger thoughts and concomitant reactions; these can be performed via aircraft sound tapes or video, watching planes at an airport, visiting a plane in a hangar, or, of course, an actual flight. It is essential that you do not divert your attention away from the situation as this will simply delay useful action. Moreover, try and uncover what you think will be the *consequences* of your thoughts; in reality nothing worse will happen, but many frightened flyers block any consideration of such eventualities. '*What if* (I panic, the engines stop, we experience turbulence . . .)?' needs to be translated into '*Even if* (I'll deal with it)', and ways of achieving this are explained later in the chapter. One way is to give yourself permission to have the feelings you are trying to prevent occurring.

The best way to identify your faulty thinking is to make an entry in a notebook whenever you feel anxious, and then try and establish what thoughts you had immediately prior to feeling that way. This is the first step in learning how to correct distorted patterns of thought and to restructure your

143

thinking so that it is realistic and appropriate. The cognitive restructuring approach which follows is adapted from the extensive clinical research conducted by Aaron T. Beck and his colleague Gary Emery, and documented in their volume *Anxiety Disorders and Phobias: A cognitive perspective* (published by Basic Books, New York, 1985).

STAGES IN DEFUSING WORRY

After recognising the automatic thoughts associated with your anxiety about flying and recording them as described, it is necessary to challenge the evidence upon which your beliefs about what might happen are based. These distorted thoughts can then be replaced with rational alternatives, after which the more pervasive underlying assumptions that mediate anxiety need to be examined.

Tuning into automatic thoughts

Automatic thoughts are perceived without prior consideration or reasoning, yet are accepted as plausible and valid. They are the substance of the *internal dialogue* or *self-talk* we all conduct with ourselves, and colour the meanings of external events. Discussion with others is generally conducted on much more logical and pragmatic grounds. Automatic thoughts have several distinguishing features from other kinds of cognitions, which will help you to identify them: they occur spontaneously, are idiosyncratic to each person, are difficult to switch off, often lead to similar thoughts, are believed regardless of how irrational, and are hardly ever noticed – so are rarely challenged or questioned. They are generally formulated in terms of absolute statements and ideals, and lead one to expect the worst. Moreover, they appear in abbreviated form – words, phrases and images – and confirm the labelling of flying as a threat and dangerous to self or aircraft or both: eg 'Flight tomorrow . . . panicky last time . . . turbulence . . . crashing . . . who would take care of the children?'

Acceptance of automatic thoughts is an excellent formula

for feeding anxiety, for such narrowing of perception excludes any possibility of alternative considerations. This cognitive 'tunnel vision' involves selectively attending to only one set of cues (negative ones) from a much larger range.

The examples below illustrate the way negative emotion is linked with flying as the result of irrational self-talk, and not from the event itself:

A
Antecedent event   Delay in departure lounge.
Self-talk   'There must be something wrong with the mechanics of the aircraft, which means it will develop problems during the flight.'
Emotion   Anxiety and feelings of vulnerability.

and

B
Antecedent event   Journey by train to the airport.
Self-talk   'I feel a bit confined here. The aircraft is even more confining. What if I panic during the flight and want to get off?'
Emotion   Anxiety, panicky feelings.

Neither event *caused* the emotions; it was the inference made by each of the passengers that only one outcome could possibly result – undesirable and distressing in both cases. However, knowing that aircraft do not leave on time for a variety of reasons (eg late from previous destination) or that what follows panic is relaxation and nothing worse, would have produced rather different emotional responses.

Assessment of distorted styles of thinking

A plane full of passengers accelerates down the runway and after about forty seconds lifts off the tarmac. Each person on board experiencing this event reacts in their own specific way.

One woman grips her seat, a priest holds his crucifix, a youth is excited, a business man looks sad. To discover why the take-off seems to trigger rather different emotional reactions it is necessary to find out what each person is thinking.

It is the youth's first trip abroad and he looks forward to the new adventure and the thrill of travelling at 500 miles per hour. The business man is concerned about the difficult meeting he has to face at the other end, and the priest always hold his crucifix – whether flying or not – for sanctimonious reasons. Only the woman who grips the arms of her seat is worried about the flight itself, and this is because she believes the aircraft is too heavy to leave the ground. She has jumped to a false conclusion in the absence of corroborative evidence. This is one category of *thinking error* involving negative thoughts that are automatic, distorted, unhelpful, involuntary, yet plausible to those who have them. The more anxious you are, the more negative thoughts you are likely to have and the more you believe them – which makes you *more* anxious.

The most direct way to determine your thinking errors is to ask yourself the following questions before finding out about how to construct rational alternatives.

1. *Are you confusing a thought with a fact?*

Example   'The stewardess is frowning and looks very serious, so she knows that there is a problem with the aircraft.'

Interpretation This is an example of *mind reading* – without actually knowing, you assume what people are feeling and why they act as they do – and also confuses a *habit* (frowning) with a *fact* (safety of plane).

2. *Are you jumping to conclusions?*

Examples   'The seat belt sign has come on so something dangerous is going to happen.'
'If I grip the arm rest very hard, the aircraft will remain stable.'

146

Interpretation A decision about cause (seat belt sign, gripping seat) and outcome (danger, aircraft stability) is made without confirming evidence; this is known as an *arbitrary inference*.

3. *Are you thinking in all-or-nothing terms?*

Examples 'The flight will be terrible'; or 'Presentation of safety instructions prior to take-off means it is a dangerous form of travel'; or 'Since I did not relax completely on my last flight, I'm a failure.'

Interpretation Dichotomous either/or – known also as *polarised* thinking – is common in anxious people trying to make sense of a threatening experience by oversimplifying it and paying attention only to the black side of things.

4. *Are you selectively attending to negative facts about flying and magnifying them while excluding all positive or neutral aspects?*

Example 'Another crash was reported in the paper yesterday, so it must be dangerous to fly.'

Interpretation Facts about flights that take-off and land safely are disregarded because they do not fit in with the preconceived idea that flying is dangerous. The media report only on the rare occurrences when there are problems, virtually never when things go right – because that is all the time, and therefore not newsworthy. Filtering out the good news and letting through only the bad, and taking selected instances out of context, ensures you will continue to worry and magnify the likelihood of disaster.

147

5. *Do you think with certainty that something terrible will happen?*

Example   'I expect disaster: What if the wing falls off, or the engine stops, or the pilot has a heart attack, or the air traffic controller falls asleep and puts us on a collision course with another plane, or . . .?'

Interpretation Here there is a demand for absolute assurance that is impossible to give. High and inappropriate standards are set which are, of course, easily violated, and confirm the self-fulfilling prophesy that flying is dangerous. This is known as *catastrophising*.

6. *Are your beliefs based on feelings rather than on facts?*

Example   'I know I will be anxious when I fly so there must be something to fear.'

Interpretation This is the belief that what you feel must be true. Feelings are used to validate thoughts (rather than the reverse). However, if you *feel* incompetent you don't necessarily have to *be* incompetent.

7. *Are you confusing a low probability with a high probability?*

Example   'I *nearly* panicked last time.'

Interpretation 'Nearly' does not mean 'did', and a possibility of something occurring is different than a probability that it will do so. Many people say they nearly panicked but *exceptionally few* ever do.

8. *Do you think your aircraft is going to have problems because you are on it?*

Example   'With my luck, we will lose an engine or two.'

Interpretation This is where you think that everything that happens is a reaction to your presence. It also extends to making comparisons with others, eg checking out who else looks nervous on the plane.

9. *Do you have a set of rigid views about how you and/or the plane should act?*

Examples 'I must behave well this time.'
'Surely, the wing of the plane shouldn't move around *that* much.'

Interpretation Setting unrealistically high (and inappropriate) standards – ie being *perfectionistic*, meticulous about detail, and making extreme or exaggerated demands of yourself in terms of 'can't, never, always, must . . .' – is bound to lead to problems, for the criteria you set are impossible to attain. As a result, when your rules are broken, you feel angry and upset.

10. *Do you blame yourself for something which is not your fault?*

Example 'I will ruin my family's holiday because I am terrified of the flight.'

Interpretation When blame and responsibility are focused on oneself for being too emotional or incompetent etc, it is easy to miss more plausible explanations. Maybe you wouldn't have had a good holiday anyway, regardless of how you travelled, but more importantly the two need not be related. Blaming others is also common, because when you are suffering the feeling is that *someone* or *something* must be responsible. This is a way of making some kind of sense out of disorder and chaos.

149

11. *Do you assume that you can do nothing to change the situation?*

Example   'I feel like a victim of fate when I step on a plane.'

Interpretation You will feel helpless if you consider yourself to be externally controlled, that is, you think that whatever you do has no influence. Other people, pilots in this case, hold your life in their hands and are seen to be in charge of your destiny. *You* don't have to control any aspects of the flight itself; that's the job of the crew. Moreover, the fact you presumably chose to fly in the first place means that at some stage you decided that you *would* reach your destination – otherwise why take the risk?

12. *Do you feel that because certain features on an aircraft don't meet expectations then the rest must be below standard?*

Example   'The cabin interior looks shabby, so the engines must be in need of servicing.'

Interpretation This is a case of generalising one or two aspects of the experience into a wholesale negative evaluation and judgement of the flight, and is known as *global labelling*. The focus of attention is often on *irrelevant* factors.

13. *Are you condemning the present on the basis of what happened in the past, maybe only once before?*

Example   'I felt unwell on my last flight, so expect I'll feel the same on this one also.'

Interpretation This is where general conclusions are drawn on the basis of a single incident, event or piece of evidence, and is called *overgeneralisation*.

14. *Are you rationalising your problems about flying?*
Example   'I prefer to travel by land or sea anyway.'
Interpretation Making *excuses* on the basis of lack of time
               or interest, or giving emphasis to an
               alternative mode of travel, reinforces
               avoidance of the problem and delays any
               possibility of resolving it.

As you read through these questions you will probably find
some which apply to you more than others. These are the
ones you will be focusing on in the next section, where a
strategy is described to help you to eliminate the distortions.

RESTRUCTURING DISTORTED THINKING

The shared belief amongst anxious flyers is that something
terrible is going to happen over which they have no control.
Beck and Emery suggest that three questions need to be
posed to facilitate a restructuring of thinking errors of the
kind illustrated above.
These are:

1. What is the evidence upon which your beliefs are
based?
2. Is there an alternative way of construing the situation?
3. What are the consequences, *even if* they happen?

1. What's the evidence?

The first step is to analyse the logic you use in interpreting
specific anxiety-provoking situations related to flying, and the
simplest way of doing this is to divide a sheet of paper into
three columns. In the first, describe the situation that evokes
anxiety; in the second, write down your thoughts about it; and
in the third, the types of error contained in these thoughts.

Situation	Thoughts	Error
Looking out of the window at cruising altitude.	It's such a long way down there. I just can't control my fear, and am sure to panic. I'm worse than anyone else on this plane and I think I'm a hopeless case. Why do I punish myself this way?	Control fallacy. Personalisation. Polarisation. Blaming. Emotional reasoning.

Now ask yourself how someone else who doesn't mind flying would think about the situation. This gives you an alternative perspective based on more rational grounds. Saying 'can't' with respect to controlling anxiety implies not knowing how to, and stifles possible progress; similarly, stating that one is 'hopeless' has the same sterile effect.

Remove the labels of personal incompetence and possibilities for change emerge.

2. Is there an alternative viewpoint?
You need to write down your anxiety-provoking thoughts and provide alternative explanations, as follows:

Negative thought	Positive thought
The cabin staff have disappeared. Is there a crisis?	They have got to have *their* tea break. If there *were* a crisis they would be in the aisle reassuring us.
Something terrible will happen on the take-off/landing.	Why should this be the one plane to crash when there are so many uneventful flights happening every moment.

It is possible to lower your anxiety level by repeatedly reflecting upon rational alternative explanations. If you are not able to think of any positive ones yourself, then ask friends or airline personnel, so that you have a more detached and objective view of the situation.

You might wish to carry around a notebook and record your automatic thoughts as they occur, and rate on a ten-point scale the extent to which you believe them: 10 = absolute conviction to 0 = not at all. This provides a measure of change over time and provides a useful barometer of your cognitive progress.

Typically, thinking errors are associated with perceived responsibility for feeling anxious, coupled with a low expectation of control, which makes change problematic. It is helpful, therefore, if you list *all* the factors you can think of which may affect the final result, along with the influences you consider each might have. Then note what control you have over each component. You will find – in all probability – that you feel you need to control a great deal that does not, in fact, need controlling. For example, a lady who never left her seat on a long flight and gripped the arm-rest the whole way realised after this exercise that it was the engine, wings and crew that kept the plane in the air, not her muscular exertions and lack of mobility; nor would her weight tip the plane sideways, despite her large size!

Some passengers feel the need to control their environment and play an active role – many businessmen fall into this category – and dislike having to be passive and not in command of everything that is happening. However, this is a personality disposition that is not peculiar to air travel, so will not be discussed further.

3. What are the consequences?

The fantasy about what might happen is consistently worse than the reality. Anxiety makes for poor utilisation of available information, especially memories of previous flights when the worst consequences did not occur, as they rarely – if ever – do. It is worthwhile to answer the following to dilute the 'disaster' to manageable proportions:

1. Pinpoint what you think the worst outcome would be.
2. Rate its *actual* severity.
3. Work out the *actual* probability of its occurrence.
4. Decide what *you* can do to prevent it from happening.
5. Sort out practical ways of dealing with it, were it to occur.

There are basically two types of concerns people have in this respect: something catastrophic happening to yourself (eg heart attack or going crazy) or something terrible happening to the plane (eg crashing or fire). In the former, so long as you do not have a heart condition and are mentally stable in other respects, there is *no* chance of becoming severely and irreversibly physically or psychologically traumatised. Even if you did get ill, relevant medication is carried on the aircraft and chances are that amongst the passengers there is a doctor on board.

The likelihood of an accident to the plane is extremely remote. Scrutiny of the safety literature is sensible for peace of mind – and *even if* it happened you would deal with it. Focus on the present, which is all you ever need to handle.

MODIFYING MALADAPTIVE ASSUMPTIONS

So far the emphasis in this chapter has been on eliminating your symptoms related to flying; now it is appropriate to turn our attention to modifying the underlying beliefs which predispose you to be anxious about any situation. These beliefs centre usually upon issues concerning *acceptance, competence*, or *control*, and represent a particular and persistent way of construing the world. The first relates to fear that you or your behaviour will be unacceptable to others, the second to concerns that you are not equal to others in coping with situations, and the third to feelings of being dominated by

154

events out of your control (or being domineered by others). Such themes emerge when you examine your automatic thoughts – in other words, when you encounter anything stressful, certain anxiety-provoking assumptions become activated that are connected to one of the above areas. For example, one client stated that 'To be criticised is the worst thing in the world' (this taps the acceptance domain); another felt that 'Success is crucial' (this relates to personal competence); and a third was insistent that she 'mustn't ask for help' (control).

These statements are generally expressed in all-or-nothing terms and determine one's reactions regarding all aspects of one's life: achievements, work, relationships, health, etc. They are used by people to protect themselves from undesirable occurrences and to promote positive experiences. The way to identify such assumptions is to think of a situation that produced discomfort in the past, similar to the distress you feel about flying, and then state the underlying belief that you were using on that occasion. One woman was reminded of being locked in a cupboard by her sister as a child and avoided confined situations thereafter, for fear of being trapped for ever. The procedure is valuable in demonstrating how memories of particular occasions in the past can interfere with the present; indeed, a person's whole life can revolve around one of the three habitual ways of thinking.

Anxious flyers can often identify the source of their major concern – it might be a critical parent, teacher or friend (if acceptance is the primary issue); failed tasks in the past (when competence is the concern); or an authoritative parent or relative (when control is the major preoccupation). Accordingly, the strategy appropriate for breaking the vicious cognitive cycle is to change your habits so you can achieve mastery of desirable goals rather than being led predictably towards the 'self-fulfilling prophesy'.

As far as flying is concerned, you need to start by paying attention to information which does *not* fit in with your beliefs – after all, the theory of flight is not a figment of someone's imagination, expressly designed to confuse anxious flyers. Set up practical exercises whereby you can test out various hypotheses – for example, approach gradually what you fear, stay there, and you will find that your anxiety actually does subside. Do challenge the causal connection between your beliefs and predicted outcomes; just because it is Friday the 13th, doesn't mean that something bad is bound to happen – such magical thinking is unproductive.

If your last flight wasn't as bad as you had expected, the tendency is to say that you were lucky this time – or that your worry *prevented* a problem from occurring. When something unwelcome happens, like turbulence, people often blame themselves that they did not, say, pray hard or long enough, and were being punished. But perhaps there is a more down to earth explanation . . .

Those who decide not to fly because of anxiety need to compare the negative feelings resulting from *not* flying with those that would ensue were they to have done so. My clinical experience shows that the shame, guilt and self-recrimination of those who avoid flying is far worse than those who are prepared to fly. In a similar way, those who do not go to their dentist when they have toothache will probably have to prepare themselves for long-term pain and discomfort in the future. Personal evaluation of acceptance, competence and control all have a relevance in keeping such problems alive, and provide the vehicle for positive change.

The way to change such assumptions is to look at the various advantages and disadvantages of holding such beliefs, and decide to replace the belief with a new, more adaptive, one. Furthermore, you can change your behaviour in relation to your concerns by, for instance, *not* reading articles about aircraft accidents (instead find out how many successful flights take place every day around the world); and don't raise the issue of aircraft safety at every dinner party or social gathering, for that too usually leads to a confirmation of negative preconceived ideas on the subject.

156

OTHER COGNITIVELY BASED PROCEDURES

The following techniques complement the cognitive restructuring approach described above and for maximum benefit should be used in conjunction with it. Go through each one carefully and you will find the combination which best fits your personal needs.

1. Organising your values

Values are the rules you live by and they influence you more than the consequences of your actions, real or imaginary. They dictate what you should, must or ought to do with respect to any situation, and the following are typical in the anxious flyer: 'I must never be influenced by fear'; 'I should go on the trip for the family's sake'; 'I ought not to go if there's any element of uncertainty'. They may contribute to your anxiety if they are conflicting – for instance, one man wanted to fly to please his boss and further his career, and liked the idea of visiting new places, but staying at home made him feel secure and allowed him to spend more time with his young family. In such a situation it is necessary to rank the values in order of importance and act accordingly; make a conscious decision about how you want to lead your life, viewing flying both as a means to an end (promotion and more money for the family in the young businessman's case) and an end in itself (for him, travelling and seeing the world). This will help you to clarify what action you need to take to achieve your desired goals.

2. Problem solving

When in the past you failed to cope effectively with your anxiety about flying, you probably felt frustrated and helpless, which makes it more difficult to select an appropriate course of action. One way of moving forward is to look at different aspects of your life – work, relationships, finances, health – and see whether you can find an instance of coping well when most others cope badly: eg you may feel very comfortable at the dentist, and if so what positive perceptions do you have about that which you can bring to flying.

Additionally, if you have more general difficulties – work is boring, not enough money, difficulty sleeping, feeling lonely – they may have a bearing on how you cope with flying. Firstly, isolate the problem situations and look at how you respond to them; then try different ways of thinking about them. Establish some goals and try and create some strategies that will help you achieve them.

An example of this is the case of the claustrophobic woman who worked in the foreign service and was administratively responsible for a far distant island. She was expected to visit it but was too afraid to travel there – this was the problem. She wanted to go and found the idea of being there appealing since she knew so much about the country and the people, but the thought of being confined for so many hours in a plane was too much to bear.

The alternatives offered were: move to a department that did not involve travel, own up to her superiors about her anxiety, or take an extended holiday so that she could work on the claustrophobic problem with respect to underground train travel and lifts, followed by a short and then a longer flight. She chose the latter goal-directed approach and it worked very well. It had not occurred to her that it was possible to tackle the flying problem this way.

3. Time management

Do you rush around, feel tired and non-productive much of the time, have too little time to relax or for personal relationships, feel overwhelmed and miss deadlines? If so, you probably need to learn how to manage your time more effectively before you try and deal with your flying difficulties. There are three stages to help you achieve this: firstly, rank your activities in order of priority and *do* the higher ones on the list first; secondly, try and delegate unwanted tasks whenever possible; thirdly, prepare a timetable that allows for *realistic* scheduling, along with giving yourself some personal space during part of *every* day. When you come round to dealing with the flying, make a definite time commitment – no more than thirty minutes daily – to do the exercises and nothing but the exercises.

4. Coping with panic

Professor Andrew Mathews, a London psychologist, and his colleagues developed a few years ago a self-talk programme to help agoraphobics defuse their panicky feelings, which has great relevance for the anxious flyer who reacts this way. The basic rationale is that when panic starts, sensible thinking stops and so by practising the statements below, adapted from the original, you will be able to redirect your feelings more positively.

1. Panicky feelings are only normal reactions that are exaggerated.
2. They are not harmful and nothing worse will happen.
3. Notice what is happening in your body *now*. Stay with the present. Slow down, but keep going.
4. Thinking about what *might* happen is unproductive. Only *now* matters.
5. Accept the feelings and wait for them to subside.
6. Monitor the level of anxiety: 10 (worst) to 1 (least). Watch the level go down..
7. Stay in the situation – this is important to progress. Do *not* try to avoid or escape.
8. Think about the progress you have made so far.
9. Now the feelings are getting less, plan the next step.
10. Now begin to concentrate again on what you were doing before.

You may wish to personalise the list so that it has more relevance to your particular situation. In any event, copy the statements and take them with you on your trip.

5. Positive self-statements

Donald Meichenbaum, an American psychologist, in his book *Cognitive-Behavior Modification* (published by Plenum Press, New York, 1977), developed a programme for coping with stress that divides the stressor – flying in our case – into four phases: preparing to fly, getting onto the plane, coping with anxiety during the flight, and a critical review after a successful flight. The following examples provide a guideline so that you can construct your own statements, which need to be rehearsed repeatedly until you are very familiar with them. In this way, they will be available to you when you need them, although you can always take a copy with you for the flight.

1. *Preparation*
What exactly do I have to do?
Whether I'm in a good mood or not, I'll do my exercises.
I am determined to get it right this time.
I will deal with any negative thoughts by providing a rational positive alternative.
Monitor my breathing and I'm in control.

2. *Getting onto the plane*
Slow down, just take it easy, step by step.
What do I have to do?
Just deal with *now*.
Use the word relaxation as a trigger to unwind.
If I get tense, I'll go into stomach breathing and do some active relaxation of my muscles.
The feelings *always* go away.
Keep organised and do one thing at a time.

3. *Coping during the flight*
Monitor my stomach breathing.
Concentrate upon what is going on in the cabin.
Deflect my negative thoughts by replacing them by their rational alternative.

It is good to accept my anxiety.
What follows tension is relaxation – nothing else.
Just focus on now.
Even if something happens, I'll deal with it.
I must expect the *best* – what I fear most rarely happens.

4. *Reviewing after the flight*
I did it and some parts went well.
I will write these down so I can remember how it actually was for next time.
I wasn't 100 per cent but it was certainly an improvement compared to before.
If I expect my next flight to be like the last I may be pleasantly surprised, but if I expect it to be better I could be disappointed.
So remember how it really was.

You can modify this list to suit your personal situation, but make sure to write down what the flight was *actually* like soon afterwards, so that you can use this information to your best advantage next time round.

6. Systematic desensitisation
This technique enables you to learn how to relax while imagining scenes related to flying that are progressively more anxiety-provoking. It involves combining the progressive relaxation exercise described in Chapter 5 with specific themes that upset you, so that you get used to, or become 'desensitised' to, flying stimuli in easy stages. First, you need to construct a hierarchy – in equal steps – of threatening situations that vary in intensity from the least to the worst thing that could happen regarding your fear.

Next, relax fully using the progressive muscular and breathing exercises, and visualise the weakest item on your list using colours, sounds, smell, touch and taste to enhance the imagery. Note how tense you get on your 10 point anxiety scale and then relax. Do not go on to the next scene in your hierarchy until you have relaxed fully, imagining the last one. Do this exercise daily until you reach the top of your list; then you need to proceed to Chapter 7 where you can continue with real-life exposure to appropriate items.

One anxious woman could not even look at a plane in a book or magazine before she did this exercise, after which she dealt with her fear of snakes in the same way.

7. Hypnosis

Hypnotic induction procedures involve *suggestion* which typically is of two kinds: (1) where the focus is on deep relaxation and (2) where the intention is to increase responsiveness to subsequent suggestions. Both direct and indirect therapeutic suggestions can be made following completion of the preliminary hypnotic induction procedure, and have been employed most in the area of weight loss and stopping smoking; but a number of my clients have also sought hypnotherapeutic help for their anxiety about flying. My view about this is that deeper physiological relaxation can be achieved by more traditional methods (like progressive relaxation), but that interest in the procedure is enhanced in the public eye by its magical connotations. Relatively few individuals in the population at large have the capacity to respond readily and profoundly to hypnotic suggestibility, and it therefore seems sensible to recommend other techniques that combine bodily and mental exercises in a more active way. Hypnosis may well be the procedure of choice for some; for those who are interested in finding out more about it, *professional* hypnotherapeutic advice can be sought to establish whether, in fact, this is suitable for you.

8. Meditation

Meditation is a variant on progressive relaxation and breathing exercises where you learn to focus uncritically on one thing at a time, either a word or sound, object or symbol. The essential component is to let distracting thoughts and images enter your mind and pass on, while returning to your chosen focus of attention. The goal is to obtain and maintain a passive attitude towards intrusive stimuli, which can be extremely effective in preventing the build-up of anxiety. Many people who meditate use a *mantra* – a preferably meaningless syllable, word or name that is repeated many times to help you free your mind of thoughts; the word mantra itself means 'to think, to liberate' and will have appealing associations for the anxious flyer who feels imprisoned by his distressing thoughts. Breathing and posture are both important to achieve a fully relaxed state of mind through meditation, and professional centres exist in all major towns where this procedure can be learned over a period of several weeks. The setting aside of two periods a day to devote to the technique is an essential requirement.

9. Thought stopping

This is a simple technique to control negative and frightening thoughts about flying, which involves concentrating on the unwanted thought – 'I feel dizzy and I'm going to panic' or 'One more bump and we'll fall out of the sky' etc – and after a few seconds deliberately saying 'Stop' under your breath to interrupt the flow. This acts as a distraction and at the same time enables you to substitute a rational, alternative positive thought in its place. It is effective in returning your thoughts to the here-and-now, and prevents the vicious cycle of self-defeating thoughts from gaining momentum.

Use it in conjunction with the cognitive restructuring and positive coping statements exercises in this chapter, and also when you are trying to do your relaxation exercise if you are affected by an intrusive noise or your mind starts to wander. You may wish to wear a rubber band on your wrist to consolidate the Stop command – this is helpful because behaviour (negative thoughts in this case) which is consistently punished (discomfort on releasing the stretched rubber band) is likely to diminish over time.

Maintaining progress

If you have digested the essence of the techniques presented in this chapter and worked hard at putting them into practice, you will probably make significant changes in your thinking, feeling and behaviour about flying. How can you maintain your progress and consolidate your gains? Firstly, be clear about what changes you made in your thoughts, feelings and behaviour to make improvement possible. Remind yourself frequently (daily) about your rational beliefs, but give yourself permission to be upset sometimes – there are many occasions when this is appropriate. Keep practising in lifts, on underground trains or when socialising, if these were anxiety-provoking to start with, and never avoid situations for phobic reasons. Schedule some time every day, however brief, to reflect on your programme and make sure you actively relax. Do not wait until you are in the mood to do any of this.

You have a large element of *choice* regarding how you respond to unpleasant events in your life. Flying, nor anything else for that matter, need ever be absolutely and catastrophically terrible. Change your beliefs and everything becomes manageable. Chapter 7 helps you to put your new coping skills into practice in simulated flying conditions, to prepare you for an actual flight.

7
Bridging the Gap – A Simulated Flight

As a rule, what is out of sight disturbs
men's minds more seriously than what they see.
JULIUS CAESAR

One of the fundamental difficulties about helping people to overcome their anxiety about flying is that flying itself is considered to be a major step to take, given that it is perceived usually as a threat or danger. The purpose of this section is to explain how to become familiar with the experiences of flying while still on the ground and to put into practice skills you have learned involving how to relax your body, and so defuse the worry associated with air travel.

It is important to remember that in general feelings *follow* behaviour, rather than the reverse. So it is necessary to confront the situation about which you may still feel apprehensive in order to demonstrate that the anxiety will subside, rather than wait until you are fully in the mood to do so. It's rather like not feeling particularly hungry, but once you start eating, your appetite emerges and continuing seems the most natural thing in the world.

An important difference about flying, compared to anxieties expressed about other situations and things such as spiders or lifts, is that aeroplanes are rather remote objects; that is, it is not so easy to arrange to take a flight as it is to travel by bus or train. It is also somewhat more expensive, and as a rule opportunities do not present themselves as frequently. Moreover, flying is often construed as a complex combination of machinery and movements and noises which is fundamentally different from other modes of transport; the medium of transmission is invisible air as opposed to rails, roads or water, which are clearly visible. Chapter 4 (Principles of Flight) explains how aeroplanes fly through air, which is a fluid, just like water, but not as dense; it is the wings which keep the aircraft in the sky, not the engines, just like gliders. For this reason it is impossible for it to 'fall out of the sky'.

The specific aspects of flying relevant to the anxious air traveller can be divided into their component parts, including confinement, view from a cabin window at altitude, jet engine noises, and movements including turbulence. These can be incorporated into a programme of graded exposure and relaxation training, so that the eventual realities of flying can be confronted in a direct and rational fashion.

There is a long tradition within clinical psychology of treating phobically anxious patients using a *prolonged graded exposure* procedure, whereby subjects are presented either in imagination or in practice with the object of concern, in sequence ranging from mildly anxiety-provoking through to the perceived worst situation. Relaxation routines and self-talk strategies (discussed in Chapters 5 and 6) are encouraged and supported throughout the presentation of the stimulus, which changes to the next one in the hierarchy once the anxiety response has been neutralised. This approach, developed originally in South Africa by Joseph Wolpe as *systematic desensitisation*, encompasses the crucial component of *confrontation*, whereby the individual works through his or her anxiety by exposure to the phobic object.

If the phobic object is spiders the stimuli are not difficult to find, but when the anxiety is in relation to air travel, one has to be more resourceful. However, lessons can be learned from the simulation of piloted flight, which is almost as old as the history of flight itself. This led in 1910 to the development of the *cockpit flight simulator* for the training and testing of aircrew, and was specifically developed to create the illusion of actual flight from the pilot's point of view. In 1979 a comparable cabin simulator for anxious passengers was constructed, and this is described below.

The progressive graded training programme for anxious air travellers developed by the author rests upon the assumption that there are specific trigger factors that lead to anxiety reactions. Flying is by definition viewed as undesirable, and the inevitable reactions set up the individual for a difficult confrontation. Flying continues to be a sensitising experience because preconceived notions about unpleasantness are selectively, or involuntarily, repeated every time. The way forward is to apply the techniques from Chapters 5 and 6 in the following situations, depending upon your focus of concern.

The exercises which follow will enable you to prepare yourself for the kinds of experiences which have made flying difficult for you in the past. The situations simulate as closely as possible sensations similar to those that you experience when actually flying, and where coping strategies (described in the previous two chapters) can be applied.

1. Audio tape of simulated flight

This contains sounds on entering an airport terminal building, stewardess announcements on board a plane and engine noises during a flight from taxying, through take-off, to landing. Discs and cassettes of flying sound effects may be available from your local library or retail outlet. While listening to these sounds it is helpful if you sit in a seat similar to the kind found on an aircraft, upright with a straight back, and wear a makeshift seat belt.

2. Movements

During an air journey one always has the sensation of movement to a greater or lesser extent, ranging from low-level fuselage vibration to more substantial changes as in banking and turbulence – all of which are normal aspects of flying.

There are several ways of experiencing such movements on the ground: travelling by train, underground, hovercraft and lift, when it is suggested that you close your eyes and imagine you are sitting on an aircraft. On train, tube or hovercraft you can heighten the realism by playing a sound tape of a flight (as in 1) on your personal stereo, if you have one, at the same time.

3. Confinement

Many people who dislike the confinement of an aircraft also are unhappy travelling by lift and on underground trains. In this case you can start by sitting in the front seat of a car with the seat belt fastened, while listening with eyes closed to the sounds of a flight on your 'walkman' or car radio. Then progress to the back seat and close the front doors. Do not leave until your anxiety rating has subsided.

You might also consider practising your coping skills in other situations you find confining, such as theatre, cinema or even a crowded church.

4. Heights

If the trigger for your anxiety about flying is connected with looking out of the window onto distant land below or at clouds above, then you need to negotiate tall buildings (in stages) or visit an area with high terrain, or find a bridge where you can get used to looking over the edge.

5. Other people

If your concern is being in the company of others and that you might panic and be an embarrassment to them, then try and find an equivalent situation in which you come under personal scrutiny, and which as a result causes you anxiety, and confront it first on your own and then in the company of other people – preferably people who don't know your true feelings otherwise the exercise will not achieve its objective.

6. Pressure on ears during take-off and climbing/descent

Try taking a high-speed lift to the top of a tall building, when you are likely to find it helpful to swallow in order to reduce the pressure on your ears.

It is recommended that the above exercises are carefully planned beforehand and that you do not tackle a situation you perceive to be *very* difficult, only somewhat problematic. Choose a friend with whom you can share the programme and who will give you support during the sessions and discuss afterwards how it went, with a view to planning the next one.

Cockpit simulation

Since the sensations of flying are in combination rather different from any other travelling experience, I realised in the mid-seventies that a simulation of the principal components – vision, movement and noises – would be of considerable help therapeutically to bridge the gap between terra firma and 'being off the ground', as so many anxious flyers put it. In conjunction with Bob Symes-Schutzmann, producer of the BBC television programme *Tomorrow's World*, who was interested in 1978–9 in doing a feature on fear of flying, a cabin simulator was conceived and built at Guy's Hospital with the help of British Airways, following a discussion of the necessary ingredients I felt needed to be included to capture the essence of the flight experience. This followed a visit to the Link-Miles *flight deck* or *cockpit simulator* company in Lancing, Sussex, where very sophisticated equipment is made for the purpose of training and testing pilots.

Flight deck simulators basically comprise a mock-up of a cockpit with accurate and fully functioning instrumentation for a variety of aircraft. All commercial airlines and the military have such equipment for every type of aircraft they fly, or at least they have access to it. Not all airlines own these, for each costs in excess of one million pounds.

The cockpit simulator is generally housed in a structure supported by hydraulic ramps that give the sensation of movement and pressure changes. A computer produces appropriate visual input, using scenes to provide reference for the approach and landing phases of flight, where visual guidance cues are essential. Traditionally, the simulator cockpit was constructed to accept a permanent display monitor or a projection device, with the image-generator system being remotely located; but nowadays the trend is for computerised scenes which give extremely realistic input of specific airports and terrains around the world, of relevance to the specific routes and destinations of the airline concerned.

The cockpit simulator enables thorough testing of a pilot's skills by introducing rare events and hazards, like an engine failure. It is encouraging to see how these are tackled dispassionately and as a matter of course. I am, from time to time and where necessary, able to arrange for clients to sit in on these sessions and find it particularly helpful in cases where someone has persistent and strongly held concerns about things like an aircraft's ability to stay in the air, turbulence, or what happens in an emergency situation such as a fire or explosion on board.

One man who for years had avoided flying because of worries regarding an aircraft's ability to reach its destination sat in on a Boeing 707 simulator and in fact 'flew' it himself between the World Trade Center towers and *underneath* the Brooklyn Bridge. He has not looked back since and now flies all over the world.

Cabin simulator

Since 1979 the cabin simulator at Guy's Hospital, the only one of its kind anywhere, has been a central element in the therapy programmes for anxious fliers. It consists of two rows of seats on a platform which pivots around the middle to give the sensation of movement (take-off and turbulence). An eccentric motor located behind the rear seats provides the kind of low-level vibration that one always seems to find during flight, due essentially to engine resonance.

On the left side there are two cabin windows and behind each there is a television monitor. These are the focus of the simulation, for during its use a videotape is played showing the view from the cabin window of a Lockheed L-1011 TriStar (overlooking the wing) during a flight from London–Paris and Paris–London. The choice of aircraft and route is deliberate since they are the ones involved in the author's Air Travel Anxiety Seminar, so that clients can have relevant exposure prior to taking the flight. Stewardess announcements and other sounds accompany the visual input – in particular noise from the jet engines – all of which give the 'passenger' an opportunity to become familiar with the changes (engine, movement, visual) that occur on taxying, take-off, climb, cruise, descent, and landing.

When clients first board the simulator they are generally asked to sit in the second row window seat so that they have the impression of being somewhat hemmed in. This is particularly useful for the claustrophobic, who ordinarily would choose an aisle seat in case they felt like leaving, and for the person who dislikes heights, for they need to get used to looking out of the window. It is emphasised that confrontation of situations previously avoided is of paramount importance, so they can rehearse their coping skills. Seat belts are also used on the simulator. These help the first-time flier to become familiar with them, as well as giving the person with claustrophobic concerns the same opportunity but for different reasons. One overweight lady, who had never flown, was worried about taking a flight in case the seat belt would not fit her. She was much encouraged and her self-esteem definitely boosted when the one she tried in the simulator did fit – only just, as it happens, although extensions would be available on an aircraft anyway.

The videotape consists of three take-off sequences from London Heathrow in wet weather; three take-offs in dry conditions from Charles de Gaulle Airport in Paris, involving pronounced banking; a whole flight in each direction; and a landing at each place. Repeating take-offs and landings enables those concerned about these specific phases of flight to find out the changes that actually occur vis-à-vis engine noise variation and aircraft movements, and leads to a reduction or extinction of their fear as a result of prolonged exposure to anxiety-provoking stimuli. For example, if some-one's fear is triggered by the noises that an aircraft makes, the different sounds are explained to them in detail and then they listen to them over and over again until they become familiar and no longer frightening.

Some clients say that they do not feel at all anxious in the simulator because it is not a real flight, but the value of such exposure is to become increasingly familiar with the actualities of flight, while feeling relatively relaxed. This facilitates increased attention to the experience and enables those who have avoided either looking out of the window or listening to the noises or resisting the plane's movements in the past, to construe the situation rather differently and less emotionally.

For instance, those who think that the noise from the engines should be unvarying or that it is dangerous for the aircraft to move about in the air, are encouraged to attend to these stimuli which are clearly presented on the simulated flight. Those who hate looking out of the window at altitude can be instructed to look for details on the ground from take-off; shifting the attention in this way helps them to feel more relaxed. Others who have never flown can find out the way flying really is prior to taking an actual flight. Such people do exceptionally well on the simulator, as well as the mentally-handicapped boy whose step-father was not sure how he would react on a flight. He was much reassured when the boy asked, when looking at the simulator video, where the boot (or trunk) was on the aircraft that he could see lining up for take-off.

Visits to aircraft

The cabin simulator brings air travel closer to the anxious flier and demonstrates that previous negative reactions about flying can be worked through effectively, while attending to the specifics of the flight itself. However, the first-time flier or the person with claustrophobic concerns may well find it of benefit to visit an aircraft of the kind in which they propose to travel, before their trip. At London Heathrow and other places it is possible to arrange to look around an aircraft, and this can be booked through the special visits department of the airline concerned.

'Happy Hour' flights

These were introduced a few years ago for the first-time and/or apprehensive flier and, subsequently, for those who, though not anxious, do not have any other opportunity to fly. In Britain they are available in the southeast (Gatwick and Heathrow), Birmingham and Manchester, and in Europe in Vienna and Oslo. They also take place in America. They represent an important development for the anxious flier.

They involve round-trip flights – ie take-off and landing at the same airport – making them both cheaper and more convenient; and most are subsidised by the airlines concerned. They are organised on an ad hoc rather than a scheduled service basis and in the UK take the form of a one-hour low altitude (about 7,000ft) flight, with a supernumerary pilot who stays in the cabin to give a commentary on each phase of the trip. Passengers are invited to visit the flight deck and explanations are given for any queries they might have.

A recent and very important development in 'Happy Hour' flights, particularly those involving the first-time flier, is to include psychological input both prior to and during the flight. This is something that I have personally been involved with, and it has proved very effective and very popular.

It is strongly recommended that you take such a flight if you have worked through this book and want to get in some practice before embarking on a longer air journey.

8

Professional Help

It's just like the real thing!
(Comment by patient who had never flown, during her first session
on the author's flight simulator.)

It is hoped that by reading the previous chapters and following the exercises and routines, your anxiety about flying will
have dissipated. But if you have not yet taken a flight you will
need to do this and put the coping skills and information you
have assimilated into practice. Remember that feelings follow
behaviour rather than the reverse, so that it is crucial that you
book a flight *before* you feel completely calm and relaxed, for
otherwise you may have a long wait . . .

Having said that, there are many people who, for a variety
of reasons, do not derive complete benefit from self-help
texts such as this one. Without supervision, it is difficult for
some to develop a systematic routine whereby a specific time
is set aside on a regular basis to do the relevant reading and
exercises. With the best will in the world, many do not seem
able to translate thoughts into action. Others get stuck or have
queries about various issues that block future progress, since
there may be no one to provide answers to what are often
straightforward questions.

Providing information on subjects about which people feel
anxious is only part of the story, as you will appreciate from
reading earlier chapters. The psychology of air travel
emphasises thoughts, feelings and behaviour a person has in
relation to facts about flying, and so this is why it is beneficial

to review these before any decision about seeking professional help is initiated. This is dealt with in the next section and is followed by details of professional help available for anxiety about flying, including the author's Air Travel Anxiety Seminars.

Dealing with blocks to progress

This book has covered many aspects of flying, including a variety of techniques to reduce anxiety, stress and tension in relation to air travel. It may be that practising a specific procedure and observing the consequences (ie positive changes) has replaced old, negative habits, such as mental worry and muscle tension. For example, it may be that stomach breathing exercises, with relatively deep, slow-paced breaths via nose and stomach, instead of short, rapid breaths via mouth and chest, enhance the sense of relaxation and well-being.

However, it is common to find that at some point in the programme old, bad habits prove difficult to dislodge. It is useful therefore, when this happens, to look at why these occur and find ways of facilitating positive change. If you have set for yourself an individual programme and feel that you are simply going through the motions without achieving anything, it is worthwhile asking yourself the following questions:

- Why are you reading the book in the first place?
- For what reasons are you doing the exercises?
- How important are these reasons with respect to other involvement in your life at the present time?
- If you are not doing the exercises, what are you doing instead, or would like to be doing?
- Is it possible to do both, and would you want to?
- If you do not give the exercises priority now, do you want to give them priority in the future, and if so when?
- What would have to change for you to continue with the exercises?
- What would be the consequence of following through with the exercises and overcoming your anxiety?

Responsibility for decisions

Depending upon the kind of person you are, it may be difficult to learn new skills when you are motivating yourself and the ultimate reward – feeling comfortable on an aircraft – seems a massive and remote goal. Distractions assume pre-eminence at such times, and so it is necessary to make a decision about whether these are excuses for not continuing or seem more attractive because of intrinsic rewards. In any event, it is necessary to set a time when you will recommence the exercises. This ensures that you are responsible for your decision, and are less likely to feel unhappy about not continuing with the original course of action.

Excuses

When the initial enthusiasm for the programme has subsided – as it often does – it is constructive to examine the reasons you give yourself about what is happening: 'I'm too busy right now with other things', 'Flying is not that important anyway', 'I'll put off the flight until next month when I'll be better prepared', 'I'm too tired', 'Flying is too expensive', 'This isn't very effective so far', 'I don't feel well enough today'. These are statements commonly made to justify a shift in emphasis away from the task in hand. While it is true that you may be busy, tired or out of funds, it does not follow that the programme needs to be interrupted because of it. It is all a matter of choice, and one has an active role in such decision making.

When such interruptions occur repeatedly over time, certain themes can usually be detected and relate to situations other than travelling by plane. For instance, some people feel that they are indispensable, and that the family or business would collapse if they took time off to do a practice flight or spent a few days away from home.

Such excuses, as explained in Chapter 6 (Dealing with the Worry Factor), are based upon faulty premises whereby absolute beliefs, such as indispensability, keep the person locked into a network of cognitive distortions that lead to

176

wrong conclusions. Typical is the example of the person who believes he cannot leave family or business or take time off, and this leads to feelings of anxiety whenever that thought is contemplated, and so the idea is dropped. The notion that family and work obligations require one's undiluted presence perpetuates the myth that taking any time off is wrong, therefore preventing any possibility for relaxation through doing so. Hence the vicious cycle ensures that the problem is kept alive. However, everyone has a right to relax and get away from work and business, stressful activities in themselves, and therefore one has to give oneself permission to do so. This is likely to succeed only if getting away (and its consequences) are construed differently and accorded some level of importance.

Pacing of one's activities is another relevant variable. Busy people tend to rush everything, and those who contemplate anything distasteful, in this case the experience of flying or exercises related to it, want it to end as quickly as possible. This is tantamount to avoidance and simply delays useful action. Slow down when doing the exercises and adopt the attitude that for that period of time there is *nothing* else more important. Try and reward yourself intermittently – by further rest and enjoyment – once you have completed a set of relaxation and stress-reduction exercises.

If you started out reading this book feeling anxious about flying and have not done any of the exercises, chances are that you are not making a serious commitment to overcome your stress reaction. Perhaps you have found that letting go, say, as part of the muscle relaxation technique is resisted for what you think might happen if you did. Stopping the exercise prevents you from finding out that nothing worse can happen were you to continue, but you need to be prepared to do so to find out.

Alternatively, you may find a particular procedure completely unhelpful; if so, simply leave it and go on to the next one. The essence of the programme is to establish a personalised series of exercises that reflect your specific needs, and there is usually a variety of ways in which desirable goals can be achieved.

Getting off the plateau

Despite having worked through all the relevant routines, some people find that their symptoms persist, which can be rather demoralising. There are those, for instance, who take on every problem they read about – one lady did not realise that others worried about engine failure so she added this to her list; others are attached to their symptoms, which can have positive consequences in helping them to get out of situations they don't find rewarding. Here, the advantage of not flying is greater than doing so; that is to say, there are 'secondary gains' to be had from keeping the symptoms alive. If this is your situation, Chapter 6 would merit re-reading.

On the other hand, claiming to be anxious about flying may signify that you are not dealing directly with some other aspect of your life and that your feelings about this are not being openly expressed. For one woman, 'I don't fly because I hate it' really meant, after discussion in therapy, that 'I don't want to travel with my husband', to whom she felt extremely hostile. This was the way she dealt with her difficult and unstable relationship. Admitting to others that you are frightened of flying can be a way of getting help and sympathy in a situation that otherwise would be difficult if you carried the burden alone. Remember that, to a greater or lesser extent, the person to whom you self-disclose is likely to have similar feelings to yours – if not about air travel, then something else.

However, if you continue to have difficulties in controlling your anxiety about flying, consider consulting a professional. It is possible to have individual or group sessions of anxiety management – available in most parts of the country by referral to a local hospital-based clinical psychologist via your own doctor – and there are now specific centres where specialist help for air travel anxiety can be obtained. One of the principal centres offering therapy for this problem is the

Air Travel Anxiety Seminar in London run by the author, which is now discussed in some detail.

Air Travel Anxiety Seminar
Background

I saw my first air travel phobic in 1976. His principal problem was with respect to heights, and as a businessman he needed to travel in connection with his work. He had to attend an important meeting in New York, otherwise his position was in jeopardy; the *QE2* was not sailing in winter and time would have been a factor anyway. It became clear at the outset of therapy that since he had always avoided flying, a graded training programme, teaching him how to relax his body and defuse the worry about panicking, would be the best course of action. At the time, the only relevant imagery available were the ones conjured up in our sessions, along with practical visits to local high buildings. This proved to be sufficient, since I later received a picture postcard from New York, posted at the one-hundred-and-ten-storey World Trade Center, on which there was a single number: 1 – his anxiety rating out of ten for the flight. My first success!

Thereafter, several single and multi-phobics passed through the Clinic, and regular National Health Service groups were established. These would run over four consecutive Mondays, followed by a flight, usually to Paris, the next weekend, so that coping skills learned during the sessions could be put into practice on an actual flight. In 1979 a cabin simulator was built at the hospital, since experience had shown that as part of the graded training procedure, it was important to give clients some exposure to the specifics of the flight experience while still on the ground. The simulator remains a central component of the therapy programme, and provides the possibility of breaking the sensations of flying into their component parts: sound, vision and movement.

In the summer of 1981 I was asked to provide the psychological input to a course for anxious fliers, called Freedom From Fear of Flying and run since 1974 (when they were first started) by Captain Truman 'Slim' Cummings, an ex-Pan Am pilot based in Coral Gables, Florida. His programmes involve four evening meetings, followed by a flight which is voluntary. It seemed to me that for a positive therapeutic outcome the flight needed to be part of the programme itself, for a number of people would decide not to fly if they had not made that commitment beforehand.

Following the experience of the Cummings' course, the Air Travel Anxiety Seminar was conceived. It took account of all the factors gleaned over the previous five years that were likely to contribute to a positive outcome, and remains the most comprehensive programme for dealing with the problem.

Programme

Although some minor programme changes have been made since the first seminar in October 1981, the format remains essentially the same.

Clients are either self-referred or directed to the seminar by airlines or health professionals. Upon registration, they are sent two cassette tapes (one on relaxation exercises, the other on flight stress control), a copy of this book, other relevant handouts and a questionnaire which they are asked to complete and return prior to the seminar. This contains details of the individual's concerns about air travel and related issues and helps the seminar leaders to structure the sessions and to take full account of everyone's needs.

The programme involves two sessions at Guy's Hospital on Day 1 and two at London (Heathrow) airport on Day 2, followed by a flight to Paris on a wide-bodied Lockheed L-1011 TriStar. The first session takes place in the tower block at Guy's Hospital, in fact on floor 29. There is a good reason for this – in spite of initial resistance about such a location by some who dislike travelling by lift or being in high places. In order to work through phobic anxiety problems it is necessary to confront relevant situations, and as far as flying is concerned, two of the greatest worries are about heights and confined spaces. In principle, these are not difficult

180

problems to resolve, regardless of how long they have been present. But avoidance keeps them alive: an approach to a lift or high place makes the person feel anxious, so they withdraw from the situation and feel relaxed again, which simply confirms their preconceived notions that confrontation would be both undesirable and intolerable.

In over 200 seminar clients since 1981, only one person has failed to make it to the twenty-ninth floor, and even she progressed to floor 14 before deciding not to proceed.

Sessions

In Session 1 the group introduce themselves and explain what their specific concerns are about air travel, what they want to achieve, and when they propose to take their next flight after the Paris trip. Clients are asked to give themselves anxiety ratings from 0–9 throughout the course, where 0 represents being totally calm and relaxed, and 9 the opposite extreme. This provides a good shorthand measure of anxiety state. Comparisons are made at different times of the day, especially between first meeting and group discussion at the end, to see to what extent the levels have changed (hopefully declined) as a function of the day's involvement. It also gives the group leaders a sensitive index of how people feel at any moment.

Following introductions, a brief discussion is held on reactions to the cassette tapes and reading material before going on to a presentation of the principles of flight. This is conducted on the lines of Chapter 4 and is intended to convey the essence of how large objects like planes get off the ground and stay in the air, along with explanations of turbulence and engine noise changes etc.

After this, an overview is given of the ways in which anxiety can manifest itself with respect to flying, and what techniques are appropriate for dealing with these. A practical demonstration follows using a biofeedback device to illustrate how deep, fast breathing has a direct effect on sweating response, as do worrying thoughts about flying. This leads on to a discussion of how to combat negative thoughts, with recommendations

181

about how to construct and use personalised lists of negative self-statements and their rational, positive counterparts (see Chapter 6).

In the afternoon of the first day, the session begins by establishing everyone's breathing pattern, to sort out the chest (thoracic) from the stomach (diaphragmatic) breathers. As you will know from Chapter 5 (Learning to Relax), when we become frightened we often slip into chest breathing, to prepare ourselves for either fight or flight, which taken to an extreme can produce the very anxiety symptoms – dizziness, light-headedness, nausea, tingling sensations – we are trying to avoid, and can compound the discomfort we experience.

Next comes the session on the cabin simulator, also based at the hospital (see Chapter 7: Bridging the Gap), which enables seminar members to take a simulated flight to Paris, prior to flying there for real. The equipment shows an actual flight (on video) from the passenger's perspective, overlooking the wing on a Lockheed TriStar. This is generally considered to be one of the most useful parts of the seminar, for it allows parts of the flight – take-off, turbulence etc – to be repeated until the coping skills that have been learned are applied effectively to bring down anxiety levels. After this, there is a general group discussion of the day's activities.

Day 2 starts at London (Heathrow) airport when a pilot shows the group around a Concorde and discusses the sounds and movements that one can expect on a typical flight, using the Heathrow–Paris route as the example, since this is the one that the group will take later in the day. Everyone is given an opportunity to put questions related to the mechanics of flight, safety, turbulence, etc, so that they can have all of their practical worries resolved satisfactorily.

An explanation is given of the visual displays and other equipment on the flight deck. Claustrophobic members often comment upon how narrow Concorde is, but when the group board a wide-bodied TriStar or Boeing 747 in the next hangar, the contrast in size fills most with amazement and a sense of comfort, since it is the TriStar in which we travel to Paris.

In the afternoon session, a senior air traffic controller at Heathrow discusses the contribution of air traffic control and takes the group through the typical processing that a flight undergoes from the controllers' perspective – once again using the flight the group will be taking as the principal example. Throughout the presentation, emphasis is placed on the central consideration of safety.

Group members then have an opportunity to listen into conversations over the radio link between controllers and the pilots of actual flights in various stages of the trip – preparing to depart, at the point of take-off, and landing approach – which is followed by a visit to the radar room, where every flight is monitored and supervised, and the 'glasshouse' from where visual take-offs and landings are controlled. Weather permitting, the group is also able to watch take-offs and landings from the roof of the control tower building. This demonstrates two main points: that aircraft movements, ie take-offs and landings, are very frequent (around 850 per day at Heathrow, across the year, averaging more than one a minute) and that the angle of take-off never exceeds twenty degrees from the horizontal, although it may seem more when one is travelling inside.

Following this last visit, the group checks in at the terminal and proceeds to the departure gate, where we board the aircraft along with all the other passengers. During the flight there is an explanation of what is happening with respect to movements and noise changes, and access is often granted to the flight deck. Furthermore, access is generally given to the galley below the cabin which necessitates a trip in a one-person lift. This is good practice for the person whose difficulties centre around dealing with confined spaces.

Upon arrival in Paris the group proceed directly to their hotel, which is usually a twenty-five-storey building on the Left Bank, close to the Montparnasse Tower – fifty-nine floors high – from which there are fantastic views. Claustrophobically inclined members are encouraged to travel on the efficient Metro to consolidate progress made so far.

The above pattern is repeated on the return flight on the Sunday and a debriefing session is held at the terminal building at Heathrow, where group members give feedback of their personal experiences over the four days, highlighting what they have achieved and felt to be the most (and least) beneficial aspects of the course. As for the future, clients are encouraged to take another flight within six weeks or so and everyone is given a letter for the captain of the next plane they travel on, introducing them and requesting a visit – for therapeutic reasons – to the flight deck. Informal follow-up is facilitated by asking all those who do fly to send a postcard to the group leaders from their destination, letting us know how their flight went. Those who, for whatever reason, do not have an opportunity to fly for some time are invited to join a future seminar group flight, or a follow-up group flight to a different destination (in the past these have included Amsterdam and Rome), so that they can continue to practise the skills they have learned and keep alive the motivation to fly.

On a more formal level, course members are sent a follow-up questionnaire periodically, which enables the durability and active ingredients of the therapy to be assessed. An annual reunion dinner is held in London in October which provides a good opportunity for past seminar members to keep in touch, exchange views and make new acquaintances.

9
Taking the Plunge – Your Next Flight

For courage mounteth with occasion.
WILLIAM SHAKESPEARE

Whether you have worked through the book systematically on your own or sought professional help for your anxiety about flying, it becomes necessary to put the coping skills you have learned into practice on an actual flight. In ideal terms, this will have been programmed from the outset, where specific areas of difficulty have been tackled on a graded basis, leading up to the trip itself. It is recognised, however, that some apprehensive fliers will have to fly with little or no advance warning because of circumstances outside their control; if this is your situation, I can only suggest that you take this book with you. Otherwise, follow the instructions below which are designed to take the uncertainty out of expectations, defuse worrying thoughts and contribute to active bodily relaxation. And use the experience to find out and come to terms with the way flying really is, rather than what you think or fear it is.

Prior to booking

Before any commitment has been made to a particular journey by air, it is typical for the apprehensive flier to entertain both positive and negative thoughts about the flight. This is the time to remind yourself of your personalised list of self-statements and to rehearse the connection between the negative and the positive in order to neutralise any ripple of

185

concern. You will remember from Chapter 6 (Dealing with the Worry Factor) that it is important to book a flight early in the programme so that you can work towards a particular goal, rather than wait until you are in the mood to fly. Otherwise you may have a long wait.

Booking

It is immaterial whether your flight is a charter or scheduled one, since both are regulated to the same high standards. The principal difference is that the charter flight is essentially a one-off trip – like the Concorde visit to Lapland on Christmas Day – arranged on an ad hoc basis when the required number of people book tickets; whereas the scheduled service runs regular flights throughout the year, regardless of numbers. This is why scheduled fares are more expensive than tickets on charter flights, not because the servicing of the aircraft is inferior. Airlines and travel agents will tell you what options are available.

When your ticket has been booked, make a list of items you want to take and gradually get these together without leaving everything to the last few hours before departure, which would simply contribute to your anxiety.

It is most helpful if, say, thirty minutes is set aside each day prior to departure for practice of self-talk routines and relaxation exercises. If the central concern has been claustrophobia, then exposure to lifts, trains, cinema, theatre, back seat of cars, is likely to be beneficial for purposes of consolidation – so long as you always leave the situation more relaxed than you entered it. Similarly, high-rise buildings and elevated country walks are likely to be worthwhile for the person with a height problem. If sleep is disrupted use the thought-stopping procedure; switch to an adaptive image or set of thoughts, focus on your breathing pattern and 'let go' of any tension in your muscles. Concentrate on the present; remind yourself that you can deal with right now, for the trip will unfold in due course, and keep to specific thoughts rather than thinking in terms of 'I *hope* that it will work'.

Try and *slow down* rather than speed up in the last few days before your trip. Structure your time with respect to priorities and make sure that the important things are done first. Whenever you get distracted by negative thoughts of the flight, take one deep breath, loosen your muscles, try and tease out what the specific trigger thoughts were and deal with them as explained in Chapter 6.

Day of the flight

Pace yourself so that nothing is rushed. Resist taking anxiety-reducing drugs and alcohol, which tend to relax the body but do nothing to change the content of your thoughts. You will need a clear head to make best use of what you have learned.

Checking in

Check-in involves presenting your ticket at the airport terminal, handing over any baggage too large to fit into the cabin for storage in the cargo hold, and being given a specific seat on the aircraft. Check-in generally commences two hours prior to departure, and if you want a particular seat it is advisable to get there early. Airport terminal buildings are usually built with departure and arrivals on different levels, and larger airports, like London Heathrow and Los Angeles International, have more than one terminal. It is important to know from which terminal your flight leaves, so that you can make your way there directly by bus, car or underground train. When you arrive at the terminal go directly to the check-in desk(s) dealing with your flight. Hand over your ticket to the person behind the counter and you will be asked whether you have any baggage for checking-in – ie any items larger than the regulation hand luggage size – for they will need to be surrendered then for storage in the aircraft's hold.

Only one piece of hand luggage is permissible in addition to duty-free purchases. Any cases heavier than 20kg, unless you are travelling first class when the limit is 40kg, carry an excess charge, which can be expensive. So remember this when you are packing. You will be asked whether you wish to have a no-smoking or smoking seat. In view of the effect of tobacco/nicotine on the body (see Chapter 2), it is recommended that when flying you choose a non-smoking seat. Preferably one next to a window so that you can monitor the visual changes that take place during flight – alterations to the wing surface structures, inclination during banking etc – and relate these to engine and other noises. It is important to do this *before* you feel totally comfortable looking out of the window, for that is one of the consequences of doing so.

It is sometimes possible to see which seats are still free by consulting the seating plan for the flight, and this makes choosing much easier. For instance, you will know which seats are over a wing and this may colour your choice, since these restrict a clear view out of the window.

Passport control and security screening

The person who checked you in will tell you at what time the flight will board and from which gate. You can then proceed directly to 'airside', the area beyond passport and security control, by following the sign 'International Departures' (obviously if you are on a domestic flight you follow the appropriate signs). At this point you will need to have your boarding pass and passport handy. A preliminary check is carried out to make sure you have a valid boarding pass, then your passport will be examined, following which you can put it away safely for it will not be required until you arrive at your destination. Immediately after this you will need to place all coats and hand baggage on a conveyor belt, and then go through an arch, for metal detection (security) purposes.

Anything you placed on the conveyor belt will have to be collected at the other side of the equipment. If you set off the alarm or an item looks uncertain or suspicious on the X-ray, then a hand search is carried out. From time to time, random searches are made, so be prepared for these. In view of the fact that security in airports has been stepped up in recent years, this is another reason to arrive at the terminal in good time, for checks can be extremely time-consuming. Their advantage, however, far outweighs their inconvenience and gives the air traveller added peace of mind with respect to control of terrorist activity.

Departure

Once you are through with the above formalities, you can either stay in the general waiting area, have a non-alcoholic drink or make duty-free purchases, but it is important that you make your way to the departure gate – details will be displayed on TV monitors and large electronic departure boards – at least thirty minutes before the flight is due to leave.

This gives you an opportunity to actively relax by doing your 'letting go' and breathing routines, and rehearsing your coping self-statements. It is essential that you focus on what is actually happening right now, rather than feed thoughts, expectations and self-fulfilling prophesies about what might take place on the flight. If the flight is delayed, adopt the attitude that you will make the *best* of the fact that you have an extra period of time to either unwind, read, walk around, make a telephone call . . . Flights are delayed for a variety of reasons, but all you need to know is that your flight will leave when everything is in order, and not before.

Boarding

Twenty minutes or so before the flight is due to leave there will be an announcement that boarding will now take place. If the aircraft is wide-bodied, those going long distances usually are, passengers sitting in the last few rows are asked to do so first, and then the next few rows are called, and so on. Those sitting at the front of the aircraft are usually boarded last – this is one of the privileges offered to individuals paying more for their seats! It is a good idea to wait awhile after your row has been called so you can miss the certain rush to take your seat. These days planes are usually boarded directly at cabin level, as opposed to steps from the tarmac as in the past, and this involves walking along a relatively narrow passageway, so

189

a delay of a few minutes will enable you to avoid the inevitable queue.

When you arrive at the entrance to the aircraft the cabin staff will ask to see your boarding card so that you can be directed to your seat. This is probably a good time to mention that you are somewhat anxious about flying, and to ask whether you can contact them during the flight if you are unsure about anything. On boarding, you will probably find that the cabin atmosphere is somewhat stuffy, but this will clear once the air-conditioning equipment is in operation, after the engines are started. You will know when it is on because it produces a characteristic noise that continues throughout the flight. Once you have found your seat, store any hand baggage you will not need during the flight, including duty-free purchases, in the overhead compartment; those items you might want – like a toothbrush on a long flight, books and valuables – stow underneath the seat in front of you. Check where the toilets are located and ask the cabin crew for a pillow for the small of your back; they are always available on longer flights.

Taxying

After the last person and item of cargo has been boarded, the doors, both passenger and cargo, will be closed, and this produces a whining noise due to the electric motor involved. A similar sound can be heard from the mechanism which controls the galley wardrobe unit, used for storing jackets, coats and suit bags. When the generator power is changed from the ground unit to the one on the aircraft, the cabin lights will dim momentarily, but other changes (noises and movements) that you might experience depend very much on where in the aircraft you are sitting. For instance, if you are seated above the wings, then the sound of electric motors which drive the flaps can be very loud, as can the noise of the undercarriage when it is retracted after take-off.

When the aircraft is taxying en route to the runway, tests of equipment take place to ensure that everything is fully functional. The first sensation when the plane moves off its stand is reverse motion, since it is literally pushed back by a tug designed for this purpose. Then the second engine is started and the aircraft moves forward under its own power, at the direction of air traffic ground control. On the way to the runway the aforementioned system checks take place – that is why you may see the flaps, slats and ailerons moving on the wings' surface.

Take-off

Several minutes later the aircraft stands at the start of the runway – or as far down it as allows a safe stopping distance if this rare occurrence should be necessary – and the pilot awaits clearance for take-off from the air traffic control tower. You have to wait for longer if you are following a heavier aircraft like a 747, because of the vortex produced in its wake. This means that the air is made turbulent and it takes a minute or two to dissipate.

During this first phase of the journey safety instructions are presented either by the cabin crew or on video, when you are told how to fasten and unfasten your seat belt, where the emergency exits are located, how to put on your life-jacket should this be necessary and to apply the oxygen mask in the rare event of a cabin de-pressurisation. Instructions concerning emergency procedures will be found in the seat pocket in front of you and it is sensible, for peace of mind, to assimilate the information presented.

When clearance for take-off has been given, the engines are opened to full power and you will experience the sensation of being pushed back into your seat as the aircraft accelerates down the runway. Among the flying fraternity, pilots are sometimes judged by their colleagues with respect to how close to the Cat's-eyes on the runway they can steer the plane without touching them. Just as on a roadway, driving over these makes for increased bumpiness, so pilots try and avoid them for their passengers' comfort.

After perhaps forty seconds – depending on type of plane,

amount of fuel carried, passenger loading and weather conditions – the pilot will 'rotate' the joystick and the nosewheel will leave the ground, followed by the main gear (the rear wheels, if you like). Depending upon where you are sitting in the cabin will determine whether you experience a sensation of climbing or falling back: those at the front will feel the former, those at the rear of the cabin the latter. The best way to neutralise the accompanying bodily sensations is to take one deep breath and make sure your limbs are loose and relaxed by doing an exaggerated version of the 'letting go' exercise.

Within about a minute of take-off you are likely to hear the retraction of the undercarriage, especially if you are seated in the middle rows of the plane. The doors which house the gear are roughly the size of two large double-beds and inevitably produce some wind resistance, along with the fact that the wheels are moving extremely fast and will create vibration in the enclosed space in which they are stored.

At this point the aircraft no longer needs full power and you may well hear a cutback of the engine tone. You will find, if you care to look out of the window, that the plane will still be flying at a positive angle to the horizontal, unless air traffic control ask the pilot to hold a particular altitude. Sometimes the power is reduced by about ten per cent in older, noisier aircraft like the Trident and BAC One-Eleven, so that noise (and therefore disturbance) for people on the ground is kept within legal limits. Concorde, which is a very noisy aircraft, flies as high as possible after take-off precisely to honour the noise abatement restrictions. Aircraft which violate these standards can be penalised since there are sound checks at strategic places on the ground, the information from which is sent back for analysis to the relevant airport authority.

Next the aircraft may well start to bank – ie turn to the left or right – in order to get onto the appropriate flight path. This is associated with an increase in engine noise since the engine power itself is stepped up to compensate for the centrifugal effect of the banking. In other words, more power is needed to maintain a particular height. When the plane levels off the power is reduced again, unless the pilot wants to increase his rate of climb. If there are clouds in the sky, these will produce very slight turbulence – a sensation which may be unpleasant due to past associations, but is never dangerous.

A whining noise may be heard if you are sitting over the wings; this is simply due to the electric motors winding in the flaps and slats, making the wing surface smooth for the cruise. Once this is completed the situation does not change until the start of the descent. However, you may find that due to cabin pressurisation you experience an uncomfortable sensation in your ears. This is easily resolved by swallowing, or alternatively you may wish to suck a sweet.

Around this time you will hear a 'bong' sound, indicating that the seat belt and no smoking signs have been turned off, which is followed by an announcement that you are free to move around the cabin and smoke if you like; but the recommendation is made that you may wish to keep your seat belt loosely fastened in case of clear air turbulence, which cannot be predicted in advance. In the past several passengers have, when their seat belts were unfastened, hit their heads on the overhead lockers and hurt themselves during an episode of turbulence, so nowadays airlines routinely advise passengers to keep them connected for comfort, safety and legal reasons. Now is the time to incline the back of your seat and put the cushion (on longer flights) in the small of your back.

At altitude the air is less turbulent, but it is possible to experience buffeting when flying through the interface between fast and slower moving streams of air. The smoothest flights of all are on Concorde, which cruises in excess of 50,000ft; but even at that level jet streams (fast-moving air at high altitudes) do exist which can be uncomfortable rather than dangerous if the aircraft confronts them. The solution is simple: the pilot can change the plane's altitude just enough to get out of the disturbance, and this is done as a matter of routine.

On a long trip, say across the Atlantic, it is possible to

detect in mid-flight sometimes the aircraft changing altitude and climbing to a higher level. This is generally because planes fly more efficiently at altitude, though it is uneconomical to do so until some of the fuel, which weighs a great deal, is burned off; in other words, it is cheaper for the airline to lift a lighter plane than a heavier one.

If you are taking a long flight it is sensible to restrict your food and alcohol intake, for these contribute to feeling physically less well both during the trip and after you land, and delay adaptation to local conditions. Try and limit your alcohol to a single glass with meals and avoid carbonate drinks completely, as gases expand at altitude and produce discomfort and wind. Remember that alcohol has twice the effect at altitude compared to on the ground, and it makes you dehydrated. Drink as much water or juice as you like, but make sure you moderate your consumption of the rest.

On a long flight the trip will be punctuated at regular intervals by meals, snacks and films, but you may find it more comfortable to ask the cabin crew not to disturb you if you are not feeling hungry or are tired. In any event, it is a good idea to walk around the cabin and this will reduce the likelihood of you developing swollen ankles and feet. It is for this reason that people sometimes complain that they cannot put on their footwear on landing; so take preventative action. Use the toilets periodically to freshen up, and men may wish to shave in order to feel revived.

From time to time, there may be announcements from the flight deck pointing out present location and other bits of relevant information, but this is left to the captain's discretion so there is a wide variation in both the quantity and frequency of broadcasts.

Descent
You will know when the aircraft starts to descend, for there is a change in engine pitch and after a while the flaps are extended so that it is possible to fly at the same speed with less power. The flaps continue to lengthen until they are

eventually fully extended, beyond the position used for take-off; this produces a drag effect which contributes in due course to stopping the aircraft on the runway when the forward thrust is cancelled. For landing approach, you will be asked to return to your seat and fasten your seat belt, as well as put your seat back into the upright position. Since winds can be quite gusty close to the ground the plane may be buffeted about in the air somewhat, but this is no cause for alarm. The same can be said of a sudden juddering motion that is associated with spoilers raised on the wing surface – these are called 'air brakes' and help the aircraft to slow down more efficiently and rapidly.

It is possible that the pilot will be instructed by air traffic control to join a holding pattern if the airport has more traffic than it can deal with right away, but these do not usually last more than about twenty minutes.

Landing

The aircraft will land first on the rear (main) wheels, followed by the nosewheel, and there will be a burst of engine noise as the reverse thrust goes into effect. This is produced by closing off the rear of the engine with metal plates, known as 'clam shell' doors because of their appearance, which you can sometimes see if you look at the back of the engine housing. They deflect the air leaving the engine both down and forwards and up and forwards, which has the powerful effect of cancelling forward thrust. The aircraft then taxis to its stand at the terminal, up till which point you are asked to remain in your seat.

Disembarking

Upon arrival at the terminal, it is interesting how so many passengers get out of their seats and block the aisle, for it always takes a minute or two for disembarkation to take place. First- and business-class passengers always have priority, and so the rest usually have to wait unless there is more than one exit door. Better to remain seated comfortably until most of the other passengers have left the cabin. If you have checked in any baggage, there will be a delay anyway before this is available from the baggage claim carousel.

Do not forget to take all your possessions off the plane. Try and find a trolley in the terminal and proceed to passport control and thereafter baggage claim, if appropriate. All signs are publically displayed in several languages and so you should have little difficulty in finding your way.

Personal debriefing

Make a note of all the aspects of the trip that went relatively well and a parallel list of the specifics that concern you still. Once you get to your destination look at these latter points and work out a routine which you can put into practice on the return journey. Positive points might be that your anticipatory anxiety started closer to the flight than previously and was not as intense, or that you started to relax sooner than you had done before, or indeed that you felt reasonably well not having taken an anxiety-reducing drug or tranquilliser pill beforehand.

Return flight

If you think that the return flight is going to be a lot better than the outbound one, you might be disappointed, but if you expect that it will be much the same you may well be pleasantly surprised. Like the outward trip, feeling apprehensive beforehand is understandable and appropriate. Just remember that your levels of anxiety did subside after a while and that so long as you concentrate on the here-and-now, the flight will unfold over time. You will always be able to deal with the present, so make the best of it. Remember which exercises worked well for you and rehearse them. Repeated practice and *making* the opportunity to fly on a relatively regular basis are the two best guarantees of a good outcome for anxiety about flying. So adopt the view that you will do whatever you can to make good something that has been difficult, rather than feed notions of avoidance and escape, which simply keep the problem alive. In other words, convert the perceived threat into a positive challenge.

Future flights

If you do not have the possibility of flying again for some time, it is recommended that you prepare a summary list of what helped you on the previous flight and consult this periodically, along with playing a tape of aircraft noises or visiting an airport from time to time to keep the images of flying alive.

Appendix I

PHYSICAL FITNESS FOR AIR TRAVEL

A variety of medical conditions require special precautions or planning prior to flying, and there are other problems where flying in not recommended under any circumstances. In fact, it is estimated that one in eight air passengers are not fully fit to travel. The following guidelines will help you to decide if this applies to you, but if you are in any doubt medical advice is strongly encouraged.

Complaints requiring particular precautions or preparations

Blood disorders Anaemia reduces your ability to tolerate an environment of reduced oxygen – ie when flying at altitude – as do circulatory problems.

Cardiovascular problems Those with angina, recovered myocardial infarction and controlled heart failure can fly safely, although ischaemic heart disease is very sensitive to lack of oxygen; this is available on board if required. Pacemakers pose no difficulties during flight but can affect pre-boarding screening equipment. Just mention this to security staff who will conduct a manual check without using the equipment.

Central nervous system disorders Epileptic attacks can be triggered in those already with the condition, due to overbreathing and reduced oxygen; also by fatigue, especially on a long journey, and irregular medication. If you suffer from epilepsy, it is a good idea to take along extra anticonvulsant medication. In those with cerebro-vascular disease the brain cells may receive less oxygen, and this is compounded by the reduced oxygen in the atmosphere, particularly on a long flight. This is the reason why elderly passengers may become confused while flying.

Ear, nose and throat problems Those with acute otitis media or sinusitis may experience pain on a flight, due to the expansion of gas trapped in body cavities. Lack of humidity in a pressurised cabin can lead to dryness of eyes, nose and throat.

Gastro-intestinal problems If you have had abdominal surgery – eg appendix removed – within ten days, it is not advisable to fly since expansion of gas in the gut can delay recovery. Similarly, if you have experienced bleeding from a peptic ulcer within three weeks, flying may reactivate this. Those with colostomies need to take extra dressings and a supply of charcoal biscuits for use in the cabin, for gas expansion leads to increased movements in the gut.

Metabolic problems If you are diabetic and inject yourself you may have difficulties if the meal is delayed. You may order a special diet and need to supervise the timing of this to suit your requirements. Changing time zones on longer flights can make travelling for the diabetic difficult; the best advice is to keep to one time schedule during the journey, and only go on to local time when you reach your destination.

Respiratory problems If you have a partially obstructed airway or other respiratory disorder – eg bronchitis, asthma and emphysema – you might well experience some breathing difficulties at altitude. However, supplementary oxygen will usually alleviate this. If required, wheelchairs and motorised transport are available in most airport terminal buildings – as they are for those whose mobility is reduced for any reason.

Tissue hypoxia can aggravate oedema – the swelling of body tissue due to excess water content, and usually characterised by swollen feet and ankles – and those who are pregnant. The best way of dealing with this is to put up your feet, if space permits, or, if not, move your legs around and walk in the cabin aisle from time to time, especially on a long journey.

Conditions where air travel is contra-indicated

These include infectious diseases, advanced pregnancy – beyond the 35th week for long international journeys and beyond the 36th week for short journeys – and those with acute congestive cardiac failure, and if you are seriously ill for any reason.

Urinary problems   If only alcohol is consumed or an inadequate volume of non-alcoholic fluids is taken, you may experience urinary discomfort. Strong coffee may lead to renal colic and is therefore not recommended.

Remember to moderate your food and alcohol intake on a flight, and try to smoke as little as possible. Eat in response to your 'stomach' clock, not just because the food happens to be served. Try and avoid foods that produce gases, eg beans, cabbage and anything cooked in fat. Maintain your fluid level, but avoid carbonated drinks. Wear loose-fitting clothes and keep on the time zone where you joined the plane until you arrive at your destination. These recommendations will help you to fly comfortably and minimise 'jet-lag' when you arrive.

Appendix II

WHAT AIRLINE INSIGNIA REALLY MEAN

Once you have overcome your anxiety about air travel you are likely to have a lot of in-flight thinking time, especially on long journeys, and in order to alleviate boredom – which can be anxiety-provoking in itself – you might try the following mental exercise as a challenging and entertaining distraction.

The idea is to compose an appropriate phrase or slogan using the letters of each airline's insignia. For example:

ALITALIA – Aircraft Landing In Tokyo. All Luggage
           In Amsterdam.
QANTAS – Question Anyone. No Trouble About
           Sleeping.
TWA   – Try Walking Across

AER LINGUS ....

AEROFLOT ....

AIR AFRIQUE ....

AIR INDIA ....

ALIA ....

ALITALIA ....

ANSETT ....

BA ....

BALKAN ....

BCAL ....

BRANIFF ....

BRITISH CALEDONIAN ....

BWIA ....

CAAC ....

CP AIR ....

DELTA ....

EL AL ....

FINNAIR ....

GARUDA ....

GULF AIR ....

IBERIA ....

INTERFLUG ....

JAL ....

JAT ....

KLM ....

LAN-CHILE ....

LIAT ....

LOT ....

LUFTHANSA ....

MALEV ....

MAS ....

AIR FRANCE ....

OLYMPIC ....

PAN AM ....

PIA ....

PSA (Calif) ....

QANTAS ....

SAA ....

SABENA ....

SAS ....

SAUDIAIR ....

SWISSAIR ....

TAP ....

TAROM ....

THAI ....

TWA ....

UNITED ....

UTA ....

VARIG ....

Index